Read &
enjoy.
Dan
Christmas 2001

A Woman's Story
of
Pioneer Illinois

Christiana Holmes Tillson

Edited by Milo Milton Quaife

With a New Introduction
by Kay J. Carr

Southern Illinois University Press
Carbondale and Edwardsville

"Illinois in the Early Days: The Life and Times of Christiana Holmes Tillson, 1798–1872," by Kay J. Carr, and "The Travels of Christiana and John Tillson, 1819–1827," by Kay J. Carr, copyright © 1995 by the Board of Trustees, Southern Illinois University

Printed in the United States of America

Production supervised by Natalia Nadraga

02 01 00 99   5 4 3 2

Library of Congress Cataloging-in-Publication Data

Tillson, Christiana Holmes, 1798–1872
    A woman's story of pioneer Illinois / by Christiana Holmes
    Tillson ; edited by Milo Milton Quaife ; with a new introd. by
    Kay J. Carr.
        p. cm. — (Shawnee Classics)
    Previously published: Chicago : Lakeside Press, R.R. Donnelley
  & Sons Co., 1919.
    Includes bibliographical references and index.
    1. Tillson, Christiana Holmes, 1798–1872. 2. Women
 pioneers—Illinois—Biography. 3. Pioneers—Illinois—
 Biography. 4. Frontier and pioneer life—Illinois. 5. Illinois—
 History—1778–1865. I. Quaife, Milo Milton, 1880–1959.
 II. Carr, Kay J. III. Title.
 F545.T57 1995
 977.3'03'092—dc20
 [B]
 ISBN 0-8093-1980-2   94-33417
 ISBN 0-8093-1981-0 (pbk.)   CIP

The paper used in this publication meets the minimum requirements of American National Standard for Information Sciences—Permanence of Paper for Printed Library Materials, ANSI Z39.48-1984. ⊗

Frontispiece: Christiana Holmes Tillson
From an oil painting owned by the Historical
Society of Quincy and Adams County

Contents

Publisher's Note

This publication marks the first publicly available edition of Christiana Holmes Tillson's remarkable story of her travels in Illinois. Tillson's original, privately printed account, appearing in the early 1870s, is virtually unobtainable, and the Lakeside Press edition of 1919, from which this reprint has been made, is a scarce item of Americana.

While Tillson's narrative and Quaife's Historical Introduction have been reproduced in their entirety, some editorial changes have been made in the interest of enhancing this account of early Illinois history. Though the Publisher's Preface of the Lakeside edition has been deleted, a new map of the Tillsons' travels of 1819–1827 has been added along with a New Introduction by Kay J. Carr. To retain the book's original pagination, a third numbering system, upper-case roman numerals, has been used for the additional material.

Illinois in the Early Days
The Life and Times of Christiana Holmes Tillson, 1798–1872

———

O N Saturday, September 14, 1823, John and Christiana Tillson, residents of Montgomery County in central Illinois, supervised the baking of bricks for the new chimney in their crude log cabin. While the bricks were cooling, he returned to his desk in the cabin and attended to the never-ending series of letters that were a part of his real estate business. She went to work in the kitchen and soon made enough cakes and pies to keep her "family" of six—that included the brickmakers and the bricklayers—satisfied for the coming week. As the day wore on, she served tea and supper to the family and to four guests; and then she climbed into the cabin's loft to make beds for her company. Finally, after their visitors were comfortably tucked in, Mr. and Mrs. Tillson prepared to go to bed themselves. Just as they were about to lie down to enjoy a peaceful night's sleep, a loud thumping noise occurred at the kitchen door. A neighbor, Joel Wright, had come with a sick horse and asked to use the Tillsons' kitchen to boil some herbs so that he might nurse the suffering animal back to health. Too tired to sleep anyway, Mrs. Tillson watched throughout the night as her husband and Wright dirtied most of her pots and pans and; incidentally, saved the horse. At dawn, Mrs. Tillson cleaned the kitchen and prepared breakfast for the crowded household. After the meal, the workers went off to spend the Sabbath with their own kinfolk, and the visitors began to leave the Tillson homestead; Judge Pascal Enos and his clerk, William Porter, went north to Springfield where they had business; W. H. Brown went south with Mr. Tillson to Bond County where they planned to catch the last of a three-day camp meeting of a group of Presbyterian ministers.[1] Mrs. Tillson was left only with Mrs. Brown, happy to be relieved of the responsibility of caring for her husband and the endless stream of company. At last, with a nearly empty house, she could turn to those household tasks that had piled up but that had not demanded her immediate attention, what with so many guests and a busy husband to feed and make comfortable. That evening, Christiana Holmes Tillson, well rested and satisfied with the course of her full day's work, bore her first child, Charles.

When she first gave birth, Christiana

Holmes Tillson was twenty-five years old. She would go on to have three more children, presumably with the same matter-of-factness with which she bore her first, squeezing their arrivals into a daily schedule that included nearly constant physical labor. Her son Charles became a lawyer and practiced in St. Louis until his death in 1865. John, the second son of John and Christiana Holmes Tillson, was born in 1825; he practiced law, joined the infantry during the Civil War and rose to the rank of Lieutenant Colonel, became a member of the Illinois legislature in 1873, and was appointed (by President Ulysses S. Grant) the collector of revenues at Quincy, Illinois. Robert H. Tillson was born in 1831 and eventually moved to New York. The Tillsons' only daughter, Christiana, was born in 1838 while the couple was visiting family in Massachusetts; it was the younger Christiana who persuaded her mother to write of her early Illinois experiences.[2] By the time she finally had the time to write about her pioneer days— forty-eight years later, in 1870—Christiana Holmes Tillson had come almost to the end of a long and fruitful life. She was born to Charles and Rebecca Briggs Holmes in Kingston, Massachusetts, on October 11, 1798. Her husband, John, was born to John and Desire Tillson in nearby Halifax, Massachusetts, on March 13, 1796.[3]

Immediately following their marriage in

1822, the young couple set off for new lives in Illinois where John had earlier journeyed as a land agent for Dr. Benjamin Shurtleff of Boston. Accompanied by Shurtleff's son, Milton, and Joel Wright (who would later take his sick horse to the Tillson kitchen), John had traveled in 1819 to the Edwardsville branch of the United States Land Office to survey and record the deed for a piece of land that Shurtleff had purchased from a War of 1812 veteran. Upon his arrival in Edwardsville, Tillson secured a job as a clerk at the land recorder's office. In that capacity, he was privy to information about the condition of government land that was available both in and outside of the Illinois Military Tract. While working at the land office, he bought 160 acres of arable land for himself on a tract northeast of Edwardsville on Shoal Creek (in what would become, in 1821, Montgomery County) and continued to record deeds for land speculators in the East. By 1832, Tillson had increased his land holdings to 844 acres in Montgomery County and was the proud owner and operator of a prosperous land office business.[4]

When he brought his bride to Illinois in 1822, John Tillson moved her into the log cabin that he had built on his first tract of land and where he had lived in a "Bachelor's Hall" with the younger Shurtleff and with Wright from 1819 until 1821. It is clear from her description of it in her memoir that Chris-

IV

tiana Tillson did not find the cabin initially inviting to her eastern sensibilities; however, she made the best of the situation and lived the next five years in the cabin as the obedient wife of a prospering businessman. With few complaints about her tiring duties, she bore and cared for her children and she cooked and cleaned for the various combinations of people who composed the Tillson household—including the female servants who worked for the family over the years. The Tillsons' use of servants was not unusual for the nineteenth century. Many families of modest means, both in urban and rural households, routinely employed young women as household servants. The practice was so widespread that, throughout the century, domestic service was the single largest occupation for women who worked outside their own homes. In her spare time, Christiana Tillson also helped her husband to keep up with his business correspondence and kept his general store when he was away from the homestead. In 1823, while his family remained in the cabin, John Tillson built another log structure in the new village of Hillsboro, where he also opened a brickyard. He was appointed the first village postmaster, an office for which he was especially suited since he had been serving as Montgomery County postmaster since 1821. In 1824, the Tillsons began construction of a brick home in Hillsboro, and they planned to move into it in the spring of 1826 but construction delays did not permit occupancy until 1827.[5]

The Tillsons lived in Montgomery County for three decades. Over the years the family prospered and grew to become one of the most influential in Hillsboro. John Tillson's business, the New York and Boston Illinois Land Company, was so successful by the 1830s that he took on a partner and opened a branch office in Quincy. He also financed and built both a grist mill and a steam mill that served the townspeople of Hillsboro and, in 1837, founded the Hillsboro Academy, the school in which his children were educated. With an increasing amount of his business being handled out of his Adams County office, Tillson began to spend more and more time in Quincy. In 1837, he built the Quincy Hotel and gave nine thousand dollars toward the founding of Illinois College. In 1843, the Tillson family moved to Quincy where the children grew to maturity and formed families of their own. John Tillson, whose father's family had a history of heart disease, died suddenly of "apoplexy" on May 11, 1853, while on a business trip to Peoria. Christiana Tillson lived for two more decades; she died in New York City on May 29, 1872.[6]

Christiana Holmes Tillson had been in poor health for the four years preceding her death but, in 1870, her daughter had convinced her to write the story of the family's early years in Illinois. The result was the accompanying work, *A Woman's Story of Pioneer Illinois*. Published originally in 1872 (or 1873) as *Reminiscences of Early Life in Illinois, by Our Mother*, in Amherst, Massachusetts, the memoir is one of only a few sources that document the role that women played in the settlement of Illinois.[7] The *Reminiscences* would have remained obscure—very few copies were printed and less than ten exist today—had it not been for the efforts of editor Milo Milton Quaife and the R. R. Donnelley & Sons Company of Chicago, who printed it in 1919. Quaife, the director of the State Historical Society of Wisconsin from 1914 until 1924 and the supervisor of the Burton Historical Collection at the Detroit Public Library from 1924 until 1947, edited forty-three annual volumes of Donnelley's Lakeside Classics, a series of small-format books that the company published and distributed free to its friends and customers at Christmas from 1903 to this day. Quaife was termed (by the *Milwaukee Journal*, at his death in 1959) the "unofficial voice of Midwestern History," and wrote or edited sixty-nine books in his long career. Christiana Holmes Tillson's memoir of pioneer Illinois was his fourth work for Donnelley and the seventeenth of the Lakeside Classics series.[8]

Quaife did very little to change the original Tillson publication and he only did so for the sake of clarity. He substituted surnames for the initials that Tillson wrote. For example, in the original *Reminiscences* she wrote of a "Mr. R." who had rented a piece of land and had made a "truck patch" to grow vegetables. Quaife inserted "Mr. Rountree" in place of "Mr. R." since it was clear that Tillson was referring to Rountree. The Lakeside book also did not include an addendum from the original that contained information about the Reverend Jesse Townsend's family (written by a Dr. Lippincott in his "Log Cabin Days"). Townsend figures prominently in Tillson's memoir and her children apparently thought that their mother would have wanted to include the snippet. The Lakeside edition also did not include a drawing of the Tillsons' brick home in Hillsboro, to which she refers in the text. Otherwise, with the exception of some simple editing that Quaife did to break Tillson's long paragraphs, the text of the 1919 book remains true to the author's original. His Historical Introduction and his footnotes aid the reader's interpretation of the original text. But Quaife's work is not entirely without mistakes. He wrote that Christiana Holmes Tillson was born on March 13, 1796. However, the census taker recorded her age as 49 in 1850; Quaife apparently confused the birthdates of John and Christiana.[9]

In his introduction, Quaife praised Tillson's work for the light it sheds on the "sectional aspect of pioneer Illinois society" and because it gives "an impressive picture of the omnipresent burden of toil laid upon the pioneer housewife." Today's readers can certainly still share in these impressions, but we should not use any excitement engendered by those impressions to over-romanticize the experiences of the Tillson family. Readers of *A Woman's Story* might remember that Christiana and John Tillson were typical people of the early nineteenth century; they were certainly wealthier than many, but so were most of the people who moved to the frontier during the nineteenth century since such a journey was always an expensive proposition. Just like millions of other Americans, they were born in the eastern part of the United States and migrated, as young adults, to the West. Just like many other people of their time, the Tillsons worked very hard to build better lives for themselves and for their children. And, just like countless other Americans, they struggled with the political and moral issues of their day. And it does not appear from her memoir that Christiana Tillson thought of her life or her experiences as unusual. In fact, her honest manner and her exceedingly low-key delivery give the book its charm.

So if readers in the late twentieth century find the Tillsons to be both typical Americans and a remarkable family, we should not look to Christiana and John to end our confusion.

However, we might look to *A Woman's Story* to explain the contradiction. The book is remarkable in the way that it illustrates the drama of everyday life in the early nineteenth century and in the way that it depicts a time when the lives of typical Americans were so different from our own. It is also remarkable in that it intimately reveals, to the modern reader, an era in which ordinary people lived through extraordinary times. Whether she realized it or not, Christiana Tillson wrote of an age in which the United States was on the verge of tremendous economic, social, and political change. In 1820, the people of the United States viewed their surroundings through a very narrow lens. But, by 1870, America would become a country in which citizens could appreciate the possibilities and the opportunities of a modern world. So, although *A Woman's Story of Pioneer Illinois* appears to be a simple story of one family's experience of frontier Illinois, it is really a book about a nation that was about to come of age.

The lives of Christiana and John Tillson might easily be used to illustrate those of many Americans in the first half of the nineteenth century. They traveled to Illinois in 1822 when all of the people of the United States were on the move, both literally and figuratively. Americans were about to change their economy from one that relied upon animal and man power for the production of mostly agricultural goods to one that used more and more machines for the output of manufactured products. This economic transformation, in its turn, brought a variety of changes to the country's social features, particularly those involving relationships between people of different regions, genders, and colors. The number of people in the United States grew from 9,638,453 in 1820 to 39,818,449 in 1870. In 1810, more than 80 percent of Americans made their livings on farms while only 3 percent worked in factories; by 1870 only half of all Americans worked in agricultural pursuits while close to 20 percent worked in industry. At the same time that this occupational shift occurred, the nation began to change from an overwhelmingly rural society to our modern urban nation; less than 10 percent of Americans lived in urban areas in 1820, but nearly 30 percent had moved to cities by 1870. Much of the new urban and industrial population was made up of immigrants, particularly migrants from Germany and Ireland who were both fleeing from the sour economic conditions in their homelands and were flocking to the increasing economic—and industrial —opportunities in the United States. While immigrants were less than 2 percent of the population during the 1820s, they accounted for 11 percent in the 1850s.[10]

Christiana and John Tillson made several trips back and forth between the East Coast and Illinois. John Tillson's initial journey in 1819, to record the deed of Benjamin Shurtleff, was uneventful; he traveled from Boston to Baltimore, by sailing vessel, then went overland to Pittsburgh, took a flatboat to Shawneetown, Illinois, and then traveled to St. Louis and Edwardsville by way of the Ohio River and the Mississippi River.[11] In the end, it was not very difficult for Tillson to journey from Boston to Edwardsville. He was not in any more danger from men or nature than a person who was traveling between settlements along the Atlantic coast. It did, however, take about a month to make the trip to Illinois and, with no modern means of communication to rely upon, it took almost as long to send or receive mail. In fact, it was the considerable time-lag in communication that made men such as Shurtleff, Tillson's original employer, reluctant to make the journey themselves.

It took Christiana and John Tillson two and one-half months to travel from Boston to Hillsboro in 1822. Their journey took them along a route that was similar to John's just three years earlier, but they were delayed because they stopped in New York, Philadelphia, and Cincinnati to visit friends. Also, instead of traveling by boat from Shawneetown to St. Louis as John Tillson had in 1819, the couple went overland through southern Illinois. And while their journey was not uneventful—as Christiana describes in her memoir—it was not particularly dangerous. By 1820 the facilities for travel from the East to the Midwest were generally developed and fairly adequate for many a pioneer.

The Tillsons probably had access to one of the many emigrant guides and gazetteers published during the period. These books outlined specific routes that one could follow to the West and told of the general facilities that one might expect to find along the way. One such aid, Samuel R. Brown's *The Western Gazetteer: or, Emigrants Directory* (published in 1817) gave accurate milleages for people traveling across Illinois from Vincennes or Shawneetown to Kaskaskia, a distance of 150 or 135 miles, depending upon the road. Other guides detailed the mileage for a land route from Eastport, Maine, on the Atlantic Ocean, to Astoria, Oregon, on the Pacific Ocean (listed as 5,304 miles in 1819) and to nearly every place that travelers might stop in between the two. (A trip along a similar route today would cover about 4,500 miles, mostly along the nation's interstate highways.) Edmund Dana's *A Description of the Bounty Lands in the State of Illinois* (published in 1819) contained a series of routes from Baltimore to St. Louis that the Tillsons might easily have used to plan their trips. Travelers who were going across southern Illinois were advised, by Brown, that they would be "obliged to camp out two or three nights." Otherwise, they could stay in the many inns that were operated by people who had leased land from the government along "public" roads.[12]

The existence and condition of Illinois roads would not have been a surprise to the Tillsons. By the early 1820s the southern section of the state was crossed by routes that were well developed and maintained, at least enough to handle wagon traffic. Many were improved roads that had been used by travelers in the Northwest Territory long before Illinois became a state in 1818. For example, portions of the eighteenth-century Kaskaskia and Detroit Trace were being used as part of the Goshen Trail, the route from Shawneetown to St. Louis in the 1820s and along which the Tillsons probably traveled.[13] Other than with the guides that they might have carried, the Tillsons would have been able to ease their journey with the informal network of acquaintances that they knew had been established along their route. It was not unusual for travelers to stay, for one night or more, with people to whom they were distantly related or acquainted. The Tillsons, for example, seemed to know of every Yankee in southern Illinois and arranged their trip so that they would pass by the homes of transplanted New Englanders. The Tillsons appear to have been typical travelers of the 1820s in at least one additional respect; when they went back to Massachusetts in 1827 to visit with their relatives, they did not simply retrace the tracks of the 1822 journey. Instead, they went north and took a boat across New York on the Erie Canal, which was just opened in 1825 and that would soon permit the extensive settlement of northern Illinois and the upper Midwest.

Christiana Tillson did not give much information about her husband's business ventures. She wrote about his extensive travel in Illinois and mentioned that she helped him with his correspondence, but she told little else about how he made his living. In fact, she is so circumspect that the reader might wonder whether Christiana Tillson sought to hide the details of her husband's profession. In actuality, John Tillson did not conduct his business in secrecy and his career was fairly representative of many men who dealt with real estate in the first half of the nineteenth century. He rode the crest of the speculative land wave for nearly twenty years and made a small fortune in the process. But then, when the wave broke in the late 1830s, John Tillson nearly drowned.

Beginning with his trip to Illinois in 1819 to record a land deed, Tillson worked as a go-between for people in the eastern states—and for some in Illinois—who wanted to invest in land. Through Tillson, these individuals would buy the land, either from War of 1812 warrant holders or from the United States government. The buyers would then hold on to the land and wait for it to appreciate before selling it to actual settlers. Eventually, land companies that were financed through the sale of stock were formed in the east to buy and sell land in huge amounts; these companies bought up land from the government and from individual speculators. The companies hired agents to scout for prospective land on the frontier and to take care of all of the necessary paper-work—paying the seller, recording the deeds, and paying the taxes—in the West.

John Tillson's career mirrored the development of the land business in Illinois. In the early 1820s, he represented individual eastern investors. He traveled throughout eastern Missouri and western Illinois to find the best land deals for his clients in Massachusetts. From June of 1820 until November of 1821 he made a series of jaunts into the bounty lands of Missouri and Illinois, keeping a journal along the way. It describes the land over which he rode and records his impressions of the people he encountered. On November 22, 1821, he and Joel Smith (who Tillson claimed he took with him "on account of his company and the advantage he would be to me with his gun by killing game so as to prevent starvation") met a band of Kickapoo near the Illinois River. He wrote that "they treated us very civilly, and asked up to eat with them." Two days later, the two travelers stayed near Lewistown with Osian M. Ross, who Tillson described as a quiet, industrious, entertaining man; he also noted that Ross was a Yankee, "or a New Yorker which is nearly the same thing."[14]

Tillson was hired as the agent for the New York and Boston Illinois Land Company in 1836 and, in that capacity, represented a group of stockholders in New York and Philadelphia. As its agent, Tillson handled huge sums of cash—sometimes as much as twenty thousand dollars—for the company, which was worth two million. He spent many days in Vandalia, the state capital until 1839, paying the company's taxes and lobbying for the Illinois legislature to give land grants to railroad companies; the railroads, he reasoned, would increase the value of the land company's holdings by attracting settlers and by providing cheap transportation for agricultural goods. Tillson urged the officials of the company to invest five hundred thousand dollars in government land along the route of a prospective railroad between the Wabash River and the Mississippi River. Hoping to profit personally, he convinced the legislature to charter the Alton, Wabash & Erie Rail Road Company to run through Hillsboro, and was named a commissioner of the railroad. Business was going so well for the land company in 1836 that Tillson made arrangements to open an office in Quincy and hired Lucius Kingman, "a person well qualified to take charge of the same" to run it as his partner.[15]

During the next year, however, John Tillson's world began to come apart. He was caught, like so many other investors and agents who profited from the great land boom of the 1830s, in the great Panic of 1837. The panic, in its turn, caused a nationwide depression that ruined businessmen across the country. In October 1836, President Andrew Jackson declared that after September 1 only specie would be received in payment for the sale of public lands on the frontier. This Specie Circular was issued in response to the increasing number of bank and personal notes that the federal government was acquiring in payment for land. The banks, many of which had very easy lending policies, did not control the number of notes that were issued to borrowers and did not keep specie on hand to back them. The president's actions caused an even larger rush, but only in the short run. The eastern capitalists eventually felt the pinch of scarce money and pulled back their investments. By the middle of 1837, land sales had declined across the Midwest; in a letter to Robert Rankin, the secretary of the land company in New York, Tillson rationalized that sales had fallen off in his two offices because "sales in the summer months will always be small, [because] at that period of time farmers have but little money on hand." But it soon became clear that he was only fooling himself. Sales continued to plummet.[16]

Then in January 1838 Tillson and the company were hit with another crippling blow. The Illinois legislature declared that land titles would no longer be issued when proof of ownership was determined through tax payments (tax titles). Owners would now have to present deeds to show that they owned their land before they could obtain titles. And since the New York and Boston Illinois Land Company had not usually acquired deeds from sellers, Tillson could no longer sell much of its land. The company was stuck with thousands of acres for which taxes had to be paid but for which it had no titles. Finally, in March 1839, the Illinois General Assembly passed a special bill that would decrease the company's tax liability by half and would buy it out for six hundred thousand dollars. Tillson had convinced the legislators to pass the law by promising to include the Quincy House Hotel as part of the deal, even though he was the sole owner of the establishment.[17] Afterward, his life would no longer be as fast-paced and he would never again cut the same figure in the community. He continued as agent for a much smaller Illinois Land Company until his death in 1853 at the age of fifty-seven.

John Tillson was a typical, albeit tragic, example of a middle-class man of the early nineteenth century. And Christiana Tillson was a typical woman of the same period. However, in many ways, the life she portrays does not fit the pattern that present-day readers might expect of a middle-class woman of the nineteenth century. She was, after all, a contemporary of Queen Victoria of England and one might think that she and women like her would have been a little more ladylike. However, history shows us that while many women lived in the Victorian age, they were not "Victorian women." When, in 1870, Tillson wrote of her early days in Illinois, she described a life of comparative isolation and of constant physical labor. In this respect, she was speaking for most women of her time. Since the overwhelming majority of American women (and men) lived on farms throughout the nineteenth century, their lives were filled with work about which most, like Tillson, rarely complained.

The stereotypical Victorian woman—pious, pure, submissive, and domestic—was the ideal, and not the reality, of nineteenth-century American society.[18] As the nation modernized and became more urban and industrial, more and more women might have approached that ideal, but the reality of agricultural drudgery was the all-too-familiar norm for most. Theirs was a patriarchal society in which men ruled and worked and women worked and worked. While men were expected to and did participate in the world outside of the home, women were expected to stay at home, raise the children, and work on the farm. In fact, a wife's willingness to labor constantly at home allowed her husband the freedom to leave the farm and engage in social, political, and economic activities.[19] So John Tillson's departure for a Presbyterian camp meeting in the next county on the eve of Christiana's delivery of their first child was not unusual. Like most husbands of the early nineteenth century, he expected his wife to bear up under the weight of difficult work so that he could carry on his career as a businessman. And she seems to have accepted her role as wife, mother, and laborer, not because she thought it extraordinary, but because she considered herself ordinary and able.

The Tillsons were a bit unusual, however, in at least one respect; they had only four children. It is true that birth rates were falling in the nineteenth century as the American population grew more urban. But the Tillson family, completed in 1838, was even below the average of 5.42 children in 1860.[20] It is impossible to tell whether Christiana Tillson suffered any miscarriages during the years of her fertility. There appears to have been sufficient space in between the births of her children for her to have become pregnant many more times; she bore her children in 1823, 1825, 1831, and 1838. However, there is another possible explanation that, if correct, would put John and Christiana right back into their roles as typical Americans of their time.

They might have been practicing some sort of birth control to limit the size of their family. That part of their personal lives, however, will have to remain a mystery to us—and rightly so.

Whatever explains the small size of their brood, it remains clear that the Tillsons were people of their time. However, in her memoir, Christiana Tillson leaves the impression that she wished she was not so typical in one area of her pioneer life. Writing in 1870, just five years after the nation had gone through the agony of the Civil War, she was clearly not comfortable with the family's personal history with African-Americans and slavery. Her story about the lives and legal fate of Lucy and Caleb smacks of both rationalization and racism. But it is difficult to distinguish her ambiguous views about slavery that she expressed in her twilight years from those she might have possessed in the 1820s.

It is not surprising that the Tillsons would be ambiguous about slavery since the people of Illinois continuously dealt with and debated the issue during the first half of the nineteenth century. As a part of the old Northwest Territory that was carved out by the Confederation Congress in 1787, Illinois was, theoretically, to be free of slavery when it became a state in 1818. However, because many of the early European settlers in the state were French and owned slaves, the Illinois Constitution of 1818 called for the protection of existing slavery and allowed the introduction of new slaves for specific purposes and for short periods of time. As a result, people were held in legal bondage in Illinois until the Constitution of 1848 finally made it illegal. Until then, a slaveowner in a southern state was permitted to take slaves into Illinois and continue to hold them in bondage.[21]

So Christiana Tillson's personal experiences with slavery in Illinois in the 1820s were not unusual. Neither, however, was her ambiguity. In fact, it might be said that Illinois was a metaphor of ambiguity on the issue of slavery during the four decades that preceded the Civil War. In the 1820s, most of the inhabitants of the state were from the southern parts of the country, and particularly from Virginia, North Carolina, Tennessee, and Kentucky. These settlers brought with them the economic and social attitudes that prevailed among their populations, including an acceptance of slavery. In fact, settlers from the slave states so dominated Illinois both demographically and politically during the years immediately following statehood, that, in 1824, electors came within a few hundred votes of calling a constitutional convention that surely would have written a document that legalized slavery.[22]

But Christiana and John Tillson were from Massachusetts and one might suppose that they would have a totally different attitude about slavery and African-Americans than that of their southern neighbors. In *A Woman's Story*, Christiana Tillson wrote of southerners in a way that was, to say the least, grudgingly respectful. She referred to them as "white folks," drew amazingly detailed and amusing character portraits of them, and contrasted their habits with those of "Yankees." It is clear that she did not consider herself or her husband to be in the same class as their southern neighbors, even though they socialized, worshiped, and did business with them. It is difficult, however, to distinguish her prejudices and attitudes of the 1820s from those of 1870 when she wrote about them. Perhaps it is good enough to say that they were probably not the same.

If Christiana Tillson was a typical northern European-American of the 1820s, then she presumably went along with the "white folks" and had little problem with the existence of slavery in Illinois. The antislavery attitudes that were responsible for her ambiguous treatment of the subject in 1870 were probably developed after the period covered in her memoir and over the rest of her life. Most European-Americans of the nineteenth century did not consider African-Americans to be their equals. And during the first three decades of the century, very few northerners concerned themselves with questions about the morality of slavery in the southern states. Abolitionists, never the majority of the northern population even up to the eve of the Civil War, did not become a major factor in the determination of American moral and political questions until the 1830s. It is safe to say, therefore, that while the Tillsons' actions concerning slavery in the 1820s are disturbing to the present-day reader, they were typical of the racism of the nineteenth century.

Through *A Woman's Story of Pioneer Illinois*, Christiana Holmes Tillson has given us an opportunity to look at the United States in the 1820s. She has presented us with a snapshot of her family, warts and all; and through it she has also given us a portrait of our entire American family in the early nineteenth century. She tells us of a time in which the people of the United States were on a precipice, about to transform their traditional agricultural country into our modern industrial nation. At the end of her life, she decided to write about her westering experiences so that her children and grandchildren might better remember the story. She must have sensed that she and other pioneers had lived through a time in which the traditional American way of life had irreversibly changed. And now, with the republication of her remarkable story, the twists and turns of history have allowed all of us to remember, too.

KAY J. CARR

𝕶𝖆𝖞 𝕵. 𝕮𝖆𝖗𝖗

Notes

1. There were no established churches in the Montgomery County area during the early 1820s. Ministers of various denominations rode circuits in which they preached to adherents in private homes or at camp meetings. John Tillson became the first male member of the Presbyterian Church of Hillsboro when it was founded in 1828. *The Semi-Centennial of the Hillsboro Presbyterian Church, March 10th, 1878, Being a History of the Church for the Past Fifty Years* (Hillsboro, Illinois: Printed at the Montgomery News and Job Printing House, 1878), 6.

2. Milo Milton Quaife, "Historical Introduction," in *A Woman's Story of Pioneer Illinois*, by Christiana Holmes Tillson (Chicago: The Lakeside Press, 1919), xviii–xix; A. T. Strange, "John Tillson," *Journal of the Illinois State Historical Society* 17 (January 1925): 719; William H. Collins and Cicero F. Percy, *Past and Present of the City of Quincy and Adams County, Illinois* (Chicago: The S. J. Clarke Publishing Co., 1905), 1:356; *The History of Adams County, Illinois* (Chicago: Murray, Williamson & Phelps, 1819), 703; "Tillson Family Scrapbook," Ms, Manuscript Collections, Illinois State Historical Library, Springfield; Records of the Bureau of the Census, Federal Population Schedules, Seventh Census of the United States, 1850, Adams County, Illinois, Reel 74, National Archives, Washington, D.C. (microfilm in Morris Library, Southern Illinois University, Carbondale).

3. Strange, "John Tillson," 715, 718.

4. When John Tillson traveled to Illinois in 1818, there were just nineteen counties in the state; the present-day Montgomery County was part of a larger Bond County that stretched all the way from the border with Wisconsin on the north to present-day Crawford County on the south. "The Illinois Bookshelf," *Journal of the Illinois State Historical Society* 38 (September 1945): 345; Newton Bateman and Paul Selby, eds., *Historical Encyclopedia of Illinois* (Chicago: Munshell Publishing Company, 1918), vol. 2, *The History of Montgomery County*, ed. Alexander T. Strange, 628; Illinois, Auditor's Office, *Land Patentees in Montgomery County Illinois From 1st: Aug. 5, 1819 through December 13, 1832*, copied by Walter R. Sanders, March

1849, Tms, Manuscript Collections, Illinois State Historical Library, Springfield, Illinois.

5. Strange, *The History of Montgomery County*, 628; William Henry Perrin, *History of Bond and Montgomery Counties* (Chicago: O. L. Baskin & Co., 1882), 223; "The Illinois Bookshelf," 345.

6. John Tillson to Robert G. Rankin, 1 December 1836, "John Tillson, Letterbook, 1836–1842, Account Book, 1836–1842," Ms [microfilm], Manuscript Collections, Illinois State Historical Library, Springfield; Strange, "John Tillson," 720–22; Strange, *History of Montgomery County*, 628, 662, 795; "Tillson Family Scrapbook;" Dorothy Bliss, *Hillsboro: A History* (Hillsboro, Illinois: Montgomery County News, 1989), 123.

7. Christiana Holmes Tillson, *Reminiscences of Early Life in Illinois, By Our Mother* (Amherst, Massachusetts, [1872]).

8. David A. Walker, "Milo M. Quaife," in *Historians of the Frontier: A Bio-Bibliographical Sourcebook*, edited by John R. Wunder (New York: Greenwood Press, 1988), 497–99; John Y. Simon, "The Civil War Years of Colonel Daniel H. Brush, 18th Illinois Infantry," in *Growing Up With Southern Illinois: The Pioneer Memoirs of Daniel H. Brush*, by Daniel H. Brush (Herrin, Illinois: Crossfire Press, 1992), XVIII.

9. Quaife, "Historical Introduction," xviii; Records of the Bureau of the Census, 1850, Adams County, Illinois.

10. It was not until 1920 that more Americans worked in industry than agriculture and that more lived in cities than in rural areas, but the trend toward increased urbanization and a greater emphasis on manufacturing was evident from the early nineteenth century. Department of Commerce, Bureau of the Census, *Historical Statistics of the United States: Colonial Times to 1970* (Washington, D.C.: U. S. Government Printing Office, 1975), 1: 8, 11–12, 105–6, 137.

11. Strange, "John Tillson," 716.

12. The most famous of the public roads was the National Road, along the eastern portions of which the Tillsons traveled in 1822. Samuel R. Brown, *The Western Gazetteer: or, Emigrants Directory* (Auburn, N.Y.: Printed by H. C. Southwick, 1817), 28; E[dmund] Dana, *A Description of the Bounty Lands in the State of Illinois: Also, the Principal Roads and Routes, By Land and Water, Through the Territory*

of the United States (Cincinnati: Looker, Reynolds & Co., Printers, 1819), 54–57, 100, 104; Josephine Boylan, "Illinois Highways, 1700–1848: Roads, Rivers, Ferries, Canals," *Journal of the Illinois State Historical Society* 26 (April–July 1933): 43; Mark J. Wagner and Mary R. McCorvie, eds., *The Archaeology of the Old Landmark: Nineteenth-Century Taverns Along the St. Louis-Vincennes Trace in Southern Illinois* ([Springfield]: For the Illinois Department of Transportation by the Center for American Archeology, 1992), 23–62.

13. Adin Baber, "Early Trails of Eastern Illinois," *Journal of the Illinois State Historical Society* 25 (April–July 1932): 49–62, map between 56–57; Rufus Blanchard, *Historical Map of Illinois, Showing Early Discoveries, Exploration, Indian Villages, Missions, Trails, Battle Fields, Forts, Block Houses, First Settlements and Mail Routes* (Chicago: The National School Furnishing Co., 1883); Wagner and McCorvie, *The Archaeology of the Old Landmark*, 31.

14. "John Tillson Journal," 27 June–2 December 1820, 13, 22, 24 November 1821, Ms, Manuscript Collections, Illinois State Historical Library, Springfield.

15. John Tillson to D. H. Nevins, 13 January, 1 December 1836, "John Tillson Letter Book."

16. Malcolm J. Rohrbough, *The Land Office Business: The Settlement and Administration of American Public Lands, 1789–1837* (New York: Oxford University Press, 1968), 222, 248; John Tillson to Robert G. Rankin, 30 September 1837, "John Tillson Letter Book."

17. John Tillson to Robert G. Rankin, 1 January 1838, John Tillson to F. Taylor, 2 March 1839, "John Tillson Letter Book."

18. Historian Barbara Welter first described the "cult of true womanhood" (or the "cult of domesticity") and outlined what many commentators of the nineteenth century felt women's natural or biological roles ought to be in "The Cult of True Womanhood, 1850–1860," *American Quarterly* 18 (Summer 1966): 151–74. Since then, historians of gender roles and relationships in the United States have confirmed the existence of the cult, particularly among urban women.

19. John Mack Faragher, *Sugar Creek: Life on the Illinois Prairie* (New Haven, Conn.: Yale University Press, 1986), 118.

20. The average number of children per woman in 1800 was

7.04. Carl N. Degler, *At Odds: Women and Families in America from the Revolution to the Present* (New York: Oxford University Press, 1980), 181.

[21.] In 1847 the Illinois Supreme Court ruled that it was illegal for slaveowners to "domicile" slaves in the state, thus upholding the *Somerset* principle that was the legal norm in the other northern states. Paul Finkelman, "Slavery, the 'More Perfect Union,' and the Prairie State," *Illinois Historical Journal* 80 (Winter 1987): 248, 256.

[22.] Finkelman, "Slavery," 252.

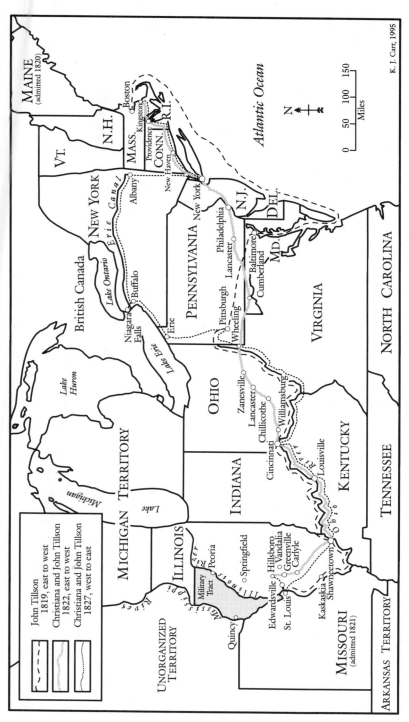

THE TRAVELS OF CHRISTIANA AND JOHN TILLSON, 1819-1827

K. J. Carr, 1995

Historical Introduction

I N The Lakeside Classics for 1918 were presented several pictures, by contemporary observers, of society and conditions in Illinois a century ago. In the present volume we return to the same field, and in the narrative of Mrs. Christiana Holmes Tillson afford to twentieth-century readers a graphic characterization of the life of the founders of Illinois as it was lived and later recorded by an acute observer of New England lineage and rearing.

Between the Illinois described by Mrs. Tillson and the present highly industrialized commonwealth of over six million people lies a great gulf. Probably there would be no exaggeration in saying that in all the material aspects of life the dweller in rural Illinois in 1820 (and *all* Illinois was then rural) if transplanted to the Illinois of today would find fewer familiar objects and more occasion for astonishment than would the rural contemporary of Augustus Caesar if similarly transplanted to the Illinois of 1820. Only by a conscious effort of the imagination, therefore, supplemented by the aid of some definite information, can the present-day reader visualize the conditions which supply the setting for Mrs. Tillson's story. An excellent picture of them can be found in the opening chapter of the second volume of the *Centennial History of Illinois*.[1] The area of settlement a century ago is sketched in the following words:

"On the day when Illinois was both territory and state its population of some 35,000 lay in two columns on opposite sides of the state, resting on the connection with the outside world furnished by the Mississippi, the Ohio, and the Wabash Rivers respectively. The population clustered in the rich river bottom, gift of the Mississippi, where Illinois history began, and in the neighborhood of the United States saline in Gallatin County. It tended always to make settlements on water courses for the sake of securing timber, water, and easy communication. Away from the rivers lay an unpopulated region in the interior of southern Illinois, where the traveler to St. Louis or Kaskaskia who preferred to cut across by road from Vincennes or Shawneetown rather than pole up the Mississippi could still stage tales of robbers, murders, and hairbreadth escapes. On the east, population had crept north, clinging closely to the Wabash, as far as the present Edgar County. On the west, settlements had reached the southern part of Calhoun County and were pushing up the creeks into Greene and Macoupin; they had also followed the Kaskaskia and its south-

[1] Theodore C. Pease, *The Frontier State, 1818–1848.* (Springfield, 1918), 2 - 3.

xii

flowing tributaries, so that settlements lay in Bond, Clinton, and Washington Counties. Elsewhere there was wilderness.

"To the north of the area of settlement lay another world distinct and independent from that to the south. The Kickapoo Indians still inhabited central Illinois, and the Sauk and Foxes, chastised in the war of 1812, but still morose, occupied a little of the territory northwest of the Illinois River—the Military Bounty Tract—though this had for some time been surveyed and allotted in military bounties to soldiers of the War of 1812. The main strength of the Sauk and Foxes in Illinois, however, lay in the territory near the junction of the Rock and the Mississippi, where Fort Armstrong on Rock Island had lately arisen to overawe them. In the territory east of them lay villages of Winnebago and Potawatomi. Among them in northern Illinois and on the Illinois and the Wabash Rivers wandered the fur traders of the American Fur Company; these came south down the lake in their Mackinaw boats each fall, dragged their boats over the Chicago Portage to the Des Plaines River, went into winter trading posts along the Illinois, from which trading expeditions were sent out during the winter, and carried their harvest of furs to Mackinac in the spring. Besides Fort Armstrong there lay in this district Fort Edwards on the Mississippi, Fort Clark at the present site of Peoria, and Fort Dearborn;

though as Indian dangers waned and Indian cessions were consummated, the forts were successively abandoned.''

Of intellectual and spiritual conditions some conception can be gained from the perusal of Mrs. Tillson's story. Whether on physical or on intellectual and spiritual grounds, one finds in it little support for the ever-popular delusion concerning a halcyon state of affairs connected with the period somewhat vaguely designated ''the good old times.'' Men and women of culture and good breeding were by no means unknown to the Illinois of 1820, but the general level of culture was, at least as compared with present-day standards, distressingly low. Mrs. Tillson's story records the reactions produced upon a refined New England woman by an environment at once predominantly southern and wholly frontier. For half a century Illinois has been regarded as a northern state. But the society known and described by Mrs. Tillson was preëminently southern in origin and in sentiment. In 1818, in a population of some 35,000, four persons out of every six were of southern stock, one was of foreign origin, and one of northern (New England or Middle Atlantic) antecedents. The northerner was prone to look with amused condescension upon the slovenly ways and provincial ignorance of his southern neighbor; while the latter repaid with interest this attitude of condescension, regarding the very name of Yankee, by which the northern man was known, as connoting qualities not to be spoken of between friends. Only by the exercise of much patience and forbearance was it possible for the two elements to associate on terms of neighborly equality. From the viewpoint of Illinois local history the peculiar value of Mrs. Tillson's story consists in the light the author sheds, sometimes even unconsciously, on this sectional aspect of pioneer Illinois society.

Equally valuable is it, however, from another point of view. The most famous son of Illinois is credited with a saying to the effect that God must love the common people, since he has made so many of them. Reasoning from similar grounds it may be asserted that God regards the female sex at least as highly as the male. But the reader of the pages of recorded history would never be led to suspect this. Why, it is not my present purpose to inquire; rather, having called attention to the fact, I wish to show the significance of Mrs. Tillson's narrative. Commonly, history is written by men and from the masculine point of view. The interests, the labors, the ideals, and achievements of the gentler half of society are taken for granted or left to the imagination. The inadequacy, not to say the injustice, of such a portrayal of history is self-evident. With unerring finger and with pen more magic than my own the latest historian of the cow country, America's last frontier, has pointed to the

woman in the sunbonnet as the supreme figure
in the history of the West:[2]

"The chief figure of the American West,
the figure of the age, is not the long-haired,
fringed-legginged man riding a raw-boned pony,
but the gaunt and sad-faced woman sitting on
the front seat of the wagon, following her lord
where he might lead, her face hidden in the
same ragged sunbonnet which had crossed the
Appalachians and the Missouri long before.
That was America, my brethren! There was
the seed of America's wealth. There was the
great romance of all America — the woman in
the sunbonnet; and not, after all, the hero
with the rifle across his saddle horn. Who
has written her story? Who has painted her
picture?"

Regretfully must we reply to the writer's
rhetorical questions, "No one." Sadly must
we admit the probability that this story will
never be adequately told. All the more, then,
should we treasure the scattering fragments
which have come to us out of the souls of our
pioneer women. If we do not know their
story, at least it is not Mrs. Tillson's fault.
From her pages we may draw an impressive
picture of the omnipresent burden of toil laid
upon the pioneer housewife, and one clear
illustration of the way this burden was borne.
In perusing it the reader should bear in mind

[2] Emerson Hough, *The Passing of the Frontier: A
Chronicle of the Old West.* (New Haven, 1918), 93–94.

the fact that Mrs. Tillson's lot was relatively favored. Her husband was a man of education and means, able to provide for her the best the frontier community afforded. Means aside, he was a man of breeding and sobriety, a leader in the business and religious life of his community. How much darker the life of many a pioneer woman might have been is but dimly suggested in such pictures as that of Brice Hanna and the more typical one, perhaps, of Jesse Buzan.

The Tillson family was of early New England lineage. John Tillson, our author's husband, was a native of Halifax, Plymouth County, Massachusetts, where his ancestors for several generations had resided. Aside from his real estate speculations, in which he soon achieved prosperity, he early became prominent and influential in Illinois, and throughout his life was active in educational and benevolent enterprises. He was the moving spirit in the founding of Hillsboro Academy, and he was also a trustee of Illinois College from its founding until his death. He was the first merchant and the first postmaster of Hillsboro, and the builder, as Mrs. Tillson relates, of the first brick house in Montgomery County. He was actively interested in religious affairs and was one of two charter members of the first Presbyterian church at Hillsboro. It is illuminating to note that such a man was very early driven by force of circumstances into becoming a slave-holder. Mr.

Tillson took some part in politics and was one of the state fund commissioners for building the railroads of the state in the early thirties. The panic of 1837 shattered his private fortune and he left Montgomery County. He died suddenly of apoplexy at Peoria in May, 1853, at the age of fifty-seven.

Christiana Holmes Tillson, our author, was born at Kingston, Massachusetts, March 13, 1796. In October, 1822, she married John Tillson and immediately set out with him for Illinois, whither he had first gone to live in 1819. Her story of the next few years, told in old age for the benefit of her youngest daughter, is the subject-matter of our volume. Mrs. Tillson is characterized in Bateman and Selby's *Historical Encyclopaedia of Illinois* as "a woman of rare culture and refinement and deeply interested in benevolent enterprises." She died in New York City, May 29, 1872.

Of the children born to Mr. and Mrs. Tillson, two should be noted here. Charles Holmes Tillson was born at Hillsboro, September 15, 1823. He graduated at Illinois College in 1844, studied law, and practiced several years at St. Louis. He died in 1865 at the early age of forty-two. A touching tribute to his memory, paid by his brother, states: "We never—running recollection back to boyhood—saw him exhibit anger; never knew him uncivil; never beheld him otherwise than pleasant, genial, considerate. This was his proverbial characteristic, and the gentle dignity that would not let itself be ruffled, parried all harsh feeling and drew to him universal love. He knew no enemies, and had none.''

Another son, John Tillson, Jr., born at Hillsboro in October, 1825, also studied law, practicing at Quincy and for a time at Galena. He entered the Civil War in the Tenth Illinois Infantry, rose to be its colonel, and was mustered out in July, 1865, with the brevet of a brigadier general. He later edited the Quincy *Whig* for a short time, served in the General Assembly of Illinois, and was for several years collector of internal revenue for the Quincy district. He died August 6, 1892.

Of the Tillson family group it remains to note only Robert Tillson, brother-in-law of our author. He was born at Halifax, Massachusetts, in August, 1800, and came to Illinois with his brother and sister-in-law on their bridal journey in the autumn of 1822. His doings at Hillsboro until 1827 are described in our narrative. For a year or so he kept store in St. Louis, but in 1828 removed his stock to Quincy on a keel-boat and started the first general store ever established there. He followed store keeping several years. In addition, he turned his attention to real estate, and with the growth of Quincy became wealthy. He died December 23, 1892, in his ninety-third year.

Mrs. Tillson wrote her narrative during the

last invalid hours of her life for the instruction
and entertainment of her youngest daughter,
who had been born too late to have personal
knowledge of the scenes described in it.   After
her death it was privately printed, apparently at
Amherst, Massachusetts, by the children for the
information of members and friends of the family.   Under these circumstances the title originally given the narrative, ''Reminiscences of
Early Life in Illinois by Our Mother,'' was not
inappropriate.   In reissuing it after the lapse of
almost half a century, because of its value as
a historical document, and for a widespread
circle of readers who have no knowledge of,
and no personal interest in, the author, it seems
better to call it ''A Woman's Story of Pioneer
Illinois.''   The original edition has long since
become excessively rare.   Indeed, we know of
the existence of but five copies, two in the
Quincy Historical Museum, one in the Chicago
Historical Society Library, one in the Illinois
State Historical Library at Springfield, and
the one made use of by the present editor in
the library of the State Historical Society of
Wisconsin at Madison.   A narrative so valuable and interesting deserves a wider audience
than it has thus far enjoyed, and the fresh
lease of life which will be afforded through
making it one of the Lakeside Classics.   We
derive some satisfaction, too, from the thought
that could Mrs. Tillson see her story in the
dignified and simple dress which is now given

it, the sight would bring a thrill of pleasure to her refined and artistic nature.

In conclusion it may be noted that the present editor has ignored the typography of the original edition, and has in certain instances made minor textual emendations which the sense of the narrative seemed clearly to call for.

MILO M. QUAIFE
Wisconsin Historical Library

MADISON, WISCONSIN

A Woman's Story
of
Pioneer Illinois

A Woman's Story
of
Pioneer Illinois

AMHERST, MASS., *June 28, 1870.*

MY DEAR DAUGHTER:

WHENEVER you have expressed a wish that I would write out some of my early western experiences, I have felt an inclination to comply with your request, but ill health and other hindrances have prevented. As writing is not my forte, I do not feel that I can produce anything which will at present interest you much; but my own appreciation of every record left me by my good mother and my dear husband makes me feel that I may leave you something which will interest you in after life, more than at the present time.

Although you have spent the greater part of your life at the West, the accumulation of comforts, and the luxuries and improvements forty or fifty years have brought, and which are there so liberally enjoyed, forbid the realization of frontier life to those who have not by stern experience passed through such an ordeal; and though we have many pleasant

3

recollections, I think, as a whole, the retrospect is preferable to the reality. Few would like to again pass through the bitterness for the sake of enjoying the remembrance of the few sweets.

Your father's date of western life was three and a half years earlier than mine. He went to Illinois in the spring of 1819, and I did not go until the autumn of 1822. He, of course, had a sterner experience of backwoods life than I had; he also had a stronger development of hope, and a most indomitable energy that carried him through all the disagreeables that came in his way. It is rare to find one so amiable in every relation in his intercourse with the world, both socially and in business transactions, who yet could be so determined and persevering in whatever he undertook to do. His boyhood and early manhood were spent with his parents on the old farm at Halifax, attending the district school winters and working on the farm in the summer. The latter — working on the farm — he performed from obedience to his father's wishes, not that he liked it. His father, at that time, was considered the richest man in that part of Halifax, and with the exception of Stafford Sturtevant, his cousin, the richest man in town. Dr. Shurtleff,[1] who was a kind of family oracle, tried to persuade his father to send him to college, but

[1] This was Dr. Benjamin Shurtleff, later of Boston, in whose honor Shurtleff College at Alton is named.

the reason given was, not that he could not afford it, but that if John went the two younger brothers would feel that they had the same right, and he might not be able to send all. So your father was sent for six months to Bridgewater Academy, each of the others being sent at the same age, and for the same length of time.

Your grandfather, John Tillson, was a kind-hearted, peaceable man, very industrious, a great worker indeed; he was a man of excellent common sense, and better educated than many of his neighbors; and with such surroundings, and his old fashioned notions, I do not think there are many who would have done more for their children.

In the year 1818, Dr. Shurtleff having purchased a farm in Chelsea, in order to settle his son Benjamin as a farmer, engaged your father to go and spend the summer at the farm, and the next winter he went into Boston to write for the doctor and to arrange business for going west the next spring. It was during this winter he attended a course of lectures on chemistry and geology, by Dr. Webster — who afterwards figured in so fearful a tragedy[2] —

[2] Dr. John W. Webster was a professor in Harvard University and in the Boston Medical College. Being indebted to Dr. George Parkman of Boston, who threatened him with loss of his position and consequent ruin, Dr. Webster invited Parkman to call at his lecture room at the medical college on Nov. 23, 1849, and in the course of an altercation over the debt struck

and he also improved other advantages which the city offered for education.

Your father's inducement to go to Illinois was in consequence of the interest at that time in soldiers' bounty lands. At the close of the War of 1812 Congress awarded to each soldier who had served in the war a bounty of one hundred and sixty acres of land, lying between the Illinois and Mississippi rivers. Then soldiers were not generally of the class to undertake the enterprise of going to a country so new; and though a few kept their parchments, and did go out to take possession of the soil, the majority sold their patents to land speculators in the eastern cities. Among the purchasers was Dr. B. Shurtleff of Boston, and your father was employed by him to attend to his business. When the soldiers sold their patent they also gave a deed, which was to be recorded in Illinois. The facilities for sending by mail, as might now be done, were so uncertain that it was deemed best to employ agents to go out and attend to the recording and locating, as the land also had to be surveyed,

him a fatal blow on the head. Instead of confessing the affair, Webster sought to conceal it by dismembering and destroying the body in his laboratory. He was found guilty of murder, sentenced to death, and hanged August 30, 1850. Because of the standing of the principals in the tragedy and the circumstances under which it was carried out, it constitutes one of the most celebrated murder cases of American criminal history.

and laid off into townships, sections, and quarter-sections. Consequently many young men of ability, employed as surveyors, agents, and recorders, migrated to what was then termed the "Far West."

Others went from a desire to go to a new country and establish themselves as farmers while land was cheap, and as was a common saying with them "to grow up with the country." Among those young emigrants were merchants, doctors, lawyers, farmers, schoolmasters, and many of them were our most cherished friends. I have now in my mind Augustus Collins, from Connecticut, who settled in what they first named Unionville, now Collinsville. He was one of your father's first and most intimate friends. Joel Wright, James Black, William Porter, Israel Seward, William H. Brown, Benjamin Mills, Samuel Lockwood, Robert Blackwell, William S. Hamilton, Edward Coles, the Ross family, of Atlas—five brothers—H. H. Snow, John Wood, Orval Dewey, Hooper Warren, Dr. H. Newhall, who settled in Greenville, and was our physician; he now resides at Galena. The three Blanchards, Samuel, Seth and Elisha, also settled at Greenville. The Leggetts, Breaths, Slocums and Allens, who settled on Marine Prairie, Thomas Lippincott[3]—I have mentioned these

[3] Many of these men rose to prominence in Illinois or elsewhere. Augustus Collins was one of five brothers from Litchfield, Connecticut, who about the

on account of their having been our acquaintances and personal friends. There are many
others that I like to keep in mind, and the
recollection of our friendly intercourse is to
me a source of enjoyment.

The two families of Townsends—one from
year 1817 laid out the town of Collinsville, Illinois.
They conducted several business enterprises and for
long were thriving Community builders. Joel Wright
was the first sheriff of Montgomery County, serving
from 1821 to 1826.

William H. Brown of New York and Samuel D.
Lockwood of the same state came to Illinois together
in 1818, descending the Ohio River on a flat boat.
Brown soon became clerk of the U. S. District Court
and lived at Vandalia, the new state capital, from
1820 to 1835. He then located at Chicago as cashier
of the Chicago branch of the State Bank of Illinois.
He was a leader in the opposition to making Illinois
a slave state, was school agent of Chicago from 1840
to 1853, and in numerous other activities served his
adopted city and state. Lockwood served in turn as
attorney general of Illinois, secretary of state, and
receiver of public moneys at Edwardsville. From
1825 to 1848 he was a justice of the Supreme Court of
Illinois, and from 1851 until his death in 1874 state
trustee of the Illinois Central Railroad.

Benjamin Mills was a native of Massachusetts who
migrated at an early day to the Illinois lead mines
and soon acquired a reputation as a brilliant lawyer
of Galena. Becoming consumptive, he returned to
Massachusetts and there died in 1841.

Robert Blackwell belonged to a family prominent
in the annals of Illinois. In 1816 he was publishing
the Kaskaskia *Illinois Intelligencer*, in partnership with
Daniel P. Cook, after whom Cook County was later
named. Mingling journalism with politics, Blackwell
became Territorial Auditor of Illinois: the firm of

Palmyra, New York, and the other from New York City — were choice acquaintances. The latter were the parents of Mrs. Hinckley. Mr. Townsend had been a flour merchant in New York, where he had failed in business, became discouraged, and his brother, a wealthy merchant in New York, entered land for him in

Blackwell and Berry were chosen state printers when Illinois became a state. This led Blackwell to make his future home at Vandalia.

William S. Hamilton, son of the famous statesman, Alexander Hamilton, removed from New York to Springfield, Illinois, in early manhood. In 1827 he again removed to the lead mine region of southern Wisconsin, founded Wiota, and for twenty years was prominent in the affairs of Wisconsin and northwestern Illinois. He joined the gold rush to California in 1849 and died at Sacramento, October 9, 1850.

Edward Coles, second governor of Illinois, was a Virginian of wealthy connections and a favorite of President Madison. In 1819 Coles removed to Illinois with his slaves, freeing them and providing each head of a family with 160 acres of land upon his arrival. Coles was the leading figure in the fight against making Illinois a slave state in the twenties, devoting to it his entire gubernatorial salary for several years. In the early thirties he removed to Philadelphia where he resided until his death in 1868.

Atlas, now an insignificant hamlet in Pike County, was laid out by five Ross brothers in the early twenties. It was the county seat of Pike from 1824 to 1833, and for a time rivaled Quincy as one of the most important points in western Illinois.

Henry H. Snow was an early resident of Alton. He was one of the three male and five female charter members of the first Presbyterian church of Alton, founded in 1821. For John Wood, who became gov-

Montgomery County, about two miles from Hillsboro. Here Mr. Townsend and family, after residing awhile at Bonhomme, Missouri, settled and were for many years our most intimate neighbors. Mrs. Townsend was a woman of uncommon energy, well educated, and fitted for more intellectual surroundings

ernor of Illinois, see note 7, *post*. Hooper Warren, a native of New Hampshire, established the Edwardsville *Spectator* in 1819, and made it the organ of the anti-slavery party in the struggle of the twenties. Warren founded the first paper at Springfield, and the third published at Chicago. In later years he retired to a farm at Henry, Illinois, and died in 1864.

Dr. Horatio Newhall settled at Galena in 1827, and practiced medicine and journalism there for several years. From 1830 to 1832 he was a surgeon in the regular army, stationed at Fort Winnebago, Wisconsin. His later life was spent at Galena.

Marine Township, Madison County, is named from the early settlement there in 1819 of a group of retired sea captains from New England and New York. Included in the number were George C. Allen and James Breath, while the location was chosen as the result of a preliminary investigating tour to the West undertaken in 1817 by Rowland P. Allen.

Rev. Thomas Lippincott, pioneer Illinois clergyman, was a native of New Jersey who came west to St. Louis in 1817. He soon crossed to the Illinois side of the Mississippi, and after several removals, in 1825 bought the Edwardsville *Spectator* from Hooper Warren. Not long thereafter he entered the Presbyterian ministry and became an influential factor in the upbuilding of Presbyterianism in Illinois. Rev. Mr. Lippincott and wife are credited with organizing the first Sunday School in Illinois, at their home at Milton in 1819. A son was auditor of the state from 1869 to 1877.

than her situation could give. Mr. Townsend
had been a handsome New York gentleman,
lacking her force of character, but refined in
manners and kind in feeling, always gentlemanly except when the blues made him gruff
and sullen. They had two children: Rosetta,
who married Andrew Braley, and Julia, Mrs.
Hinckley. Both Rosetta and Julia spent a
great part of their time in our family, calling
your father and myself papa and mamma, while
Charles and John had a "Parter Willie" and
a "Mubber Townsend," all feeling that they
had two fathers and two mothers.

Of the other Townsend family you will find
a record in Dr. Lippincott's *Log Cabin Days
in the West.* Both Mr. and Mrs. Jesse Townsend and their children, with Dr. Perrine and
family, were our intimate friends. But to
return to your father's start for the West:

In 1819 going to Illinois was more of an
event than a trip now would be to the most re-
mote part of the habitable globe. No railroads
and steamboats to annihilate time and distance
and the good people of Halifax were furnished
with a new topic of conversation when it was
known that John Tillson was going to Illinois,
some approving, while others thought it a wild
undertaking, and that he would find it so before
he was half through his journey. He started
from Boston, taking passage on a sailing vessel
for Baltimore. His companions in travel were
Moses Hallet and wife, Cape Coders. They

were married a few days previous to starting for the West, and the honeymoon was divided between the seasickness of the first and the landsickness of the latter part of their journey. Mr. Hallet, an honest and highminded Yankee, but good-natured and mischievous, amused us with the incidents of their travel when he visited your father in after years. I do not remember much of their trip across the mountains, there being then no National Road, but at Pittsburgh I think they took a flatboat to Shawneetown.

Your father's first business on reaching Illinois, where he arrived in June, 1819, was with the recorder of deeds at Edwardsville. I think he left his papers with Mr. Randall, the recorder, and went to Missouri on land business. When he returned, the office was so much crowded with previous business that nothing could be done for him, and Mr. Randall proposed that he should enter the office as clerk and write until his deeds were recorded, which offer he accepted. Mr. Randall had two other young men employed as clerks; one now the Hon. Hiram Rountree[4] of Hillsboro, the other Joel Wright Esq., of Canton, Fulton County, Illinois. While they were together

[4] Judge Hiram Rountree was born in North Carolina in 1794 and died in 1873. He came to Illinois in 1817, having studied law at Bowling Green, Kentucky. In 1821 he assisted in organizing Montgomery County, and for upwards of half a century was an official of the county and one of its most influential citizens.

John Tillson
From an oil painting owned by the
Historical Society of Quincy and Adams County

in the office during the winter of 1819–20,
two or three young men called to see if Mr.
Randall would buy their land. They were
specimens of the many disappointed Yankees
who had gone west, spent all their money for
land, and had not the means of getting back
to commence the world anew. The three
clerks, from compassion for the poor fellows,
each bought a quarter section of land, paid
them, and sent them home to their mammas
rejoicing. The land was situated in territory
belonging either to Bond or Madison County,
forty miles north of Edwardsville.

Towards spring, having a little ease from
business, they started in search of their new
possessions, expecting to make the journey in
a day, but getting lost on a large prairie were
obliged to camp, and were several days in
finding what afterwards became their home.
Mr. Rountree and Mr. Wright found their
land just as nature had made it. On your
father's quarter section a squatter had made
what was then termed "an improvement,"
said improvement consisting of a few acres
enclosed by a rail fence, with a cabin and
smoke-house in the center. The squatter,
when what they called the "rale owner"
made his appearance, expected to be paid well
for all his "improvements," and woe for the
Yankee who did not "pony up well" to the
squatter. Your father had no trouble with
his occupant. The lord of the soil was no less

a man than Commodore Yoakum, the best hunter, the life of the corn-shuckings, the best "corner man" at a log-cabin raising. His house was always open to neighbors and his friends—though a little like Madam Blaze's hand.

At his meetings—Hard-shell Baptists— no one could raise their voice louder in the "hymes," Old Grimes being his favorite tune. After the "hymes" he would gird himself with a towel, and with a tin wash-basin of water go around and wash the feet of the brethren and sisters with a good grace, and with as much apparent zest as when he took good aim and brought down a number of prairie chickens at one shot. Being so clever and handy while he always maintained an air of command, the boys had honored him with the title of Commodore, which seemed to amuse and please him exceedingly. The Commodore was a large, black-eyed, black-bearded, dark-skinned Tennesseean. He had had a grand or great-grandfather who had been a large land-owner and slave-holder, and that circumstance, with the fact that the tract where his ancestors resided had been distinguished and still bore the name of Yoakum Station, combining with his large development of esteem, rendered our Commodore, in his own estimation, second to no man.

On returning to Edwardsville your father found quite a large commission of new business from Boston and New York, which decided him about spending another year. He made the arrangement that his letters should be addressed at Edwardsville, having agreed with Mr. Randall that he should record his own deeds there, and when a package was completed he would ride out to the farm and superintend and work at "the improvement."

In the autumn of 1820, in company with a surveyor, he went into Missouri, was taken with chills and fever, but succeeded in reaching his friend Hallet's house, where he was well nursed and cared for. The next winter, 1820-21, he, with Israel Seward, Hiram Rountree, and Eleazer Townsend, went with a petition to the legislature, then in session, asking that a new county (Montgomery) be formed north of Fayette and Bond, their lands being within the new county.[5] Their petition was granted, and in the spring Mr. Seward received the appointment of probate judge; Mr. Rountree was appointed county clerk, Mr. Wright, sheriff, and your father was made

[5] Montgomery County was erected by act of the legislature early in 1821. After some bickering the present site of Hillsboro was selected for the county seat in 1823. The land thus chosen was not then entered. The story is told that after some delay the county-seat commissioners heard of a man named Coffey living at some distance who had fifty dollars in money. They thereupon sent for him and induced him to enter the land. Coffey did so, donated twenty acres for public buildings, and proceeded to lay out the town of Hillsboro on the remainder of the tract

postmaster of the county, but there being no mail route established within twenty miles of their county seat, the expense of the mail for that distance devolved on the postmaster. This your father turned into a convenience, and there being no regular place of worship in his own neighborhood he would ride down to Greenville on Saturday afternoon and return on Monday with the county mail in his pocket; sometimes in his hat. At that time his business was almost entirely done through correspondence, and as every letter from New York or Boston called for a postage of twenty-five cents, and his business was still increasing, the franking privilege was to him a great consideration.

He found at Greenville the Massachusetts family of Blanchards, Birge, the postmaster, a Vermonter, Dr. Newhall, a native of Lynn, Mass., a graduate of Harvard and a classmate of Uncle Charles Briggs; also Benjamin Mills, a lawyer of note, who, with Dr. Newhall, afterwards removed to Galena, and Dr. Perrine, who married Ann, a daughter of the Rev. Jesse Townsend, altogether forming a very pleasant circle.

The good people of Greenville, wishing to improve their music, had started a singing class. They requested your father to meet with them every Saturday night, when he came down for the mail, and also to become leader of the choir, which he did. Being thus

established as singing master, farmer, land
agent, county treasurer and postmaster, his
ties seemed strengthening in Illinois, and he
changed his address from Edwardsville to
what was then Hamilton, afterwards Hillsboro,
and took possession of his cabin. Here he,
with Wright and Rountree, kept "Bachelor's
Hall," a small commencement at first, but a
nucleus for all the sick, the homesick, newly
arrived, and errant bachelors generally. All
sought and took shelter at "Bachelor's Hall."
Among the arrivals that winter were Milton
Shurtleff from Carver, and William Porter
from Middleboro. Porter was a handsome,
well educated young man, of a character quite
the reverse of Shurtleff. Alas! for poor Porter; I will speak of him hereafter. Mr. John
Simpson, a young gentleman from Boston,
made them a visit, and entered into all their
labors and enjoyments. On leaving he handed
your father a note without any remark. On
opening he found it contained a list of articles
that Simpson had brought out for his own convenience. Each article had the price attached
to it, and enclosed in the note was a very
valuable gold chain, with the price marked.
Your father looked over the note and enclosed
the amount of money set on the whole, and
putting the gold chain with the cash, handed
it back to him. The thing was so delicately
done that I have always remembered it, and I
found two years afterward, when I went west,

great convenience in some of the articles Mr. Simpson had left. The cot bedstead and narrow mattress was just what I needed for my little Dutch girl. A very nice bottle-case with cut-glass bottles and tumblers, and a few books I appreciated. The nicest thing was a most complete gentleman's dressing-case, which, strange to say, had survived the two years' deprivation of all the bachelors who honored the cabin by making themselves at home. Mr. Simpson and your father remained friends as long as Mr. Simpson lived. It seems strange that those who went west at that time, however discouraging their efforts might have been, when they returned to the East cherished a lingering desire for another attempt, and it was very common for them to return for a second experience. Such was the tragic story of Mr. Simpson.

Sometime in 1821 your father went on an exploring trip, his object being to survey and report to non-residents the condition of their lands lying between the Mississippi and Illinois Rivers; he took with him a hunter and two other men. They were out three weeks, and only two or three times did it fall to their lot to find a shelter for the night other than the lone forest or the broad prairie. They would generally find some spring or water course, where they would build their fire. The hunter, who acted as caterer and cook, would cut slices from the game that he had secured through

the day, cooking them on sharp sticks before
the fire, one end being driven in the ground,
would soon treat them to a palatable meal, and
when their repast was ended they would enjoy
a sound sleep, finding their saddles when con-
verted into pillows as useful as the famous
chest of drawers, which also was a bed at
night. As the red brethren have a liking for
good horses, and the prairie wolves a keen
scent for a good lunch, I believe they found it
necessary to keep a kind of gander watch, one
standing sentinel while the others slept.

They crossed the Illinois near the mouth.
At that time, I think, there was but one county
on the military tract and what now constitutes
Calhoun and Pike was all one county, under
the name of Pike.[6] John Shaw, one of the
first settlers, and a great politician and fond
of rule, made himself conspicuous in Pike at
that time. He was a large, dark-complexioned
man, with a power to lead, and to gather about
him warm friends, while his peculiarities were
such as to insure for him an equal amount of
antagonism. He—by those not in subjection
to him—was known as "The Black Prince of
the Kingdom of Pike." Your father partook
of the hospitality of his bachelor cabin, which

[6] Pike County was organized in 1821, being one of
the first counties erected after the admission of Illinois to statehood. Its original boundaries included
all of Illinois north and west of the Illinois and its
affluent, the Kankakee.

was returned in full after we were housekeepers, as we chanced to be on his road to
the seat of government.   He had been elected
from his ''Kingdom of Pike'' to the legislature,
where he was always known as a troublesome
member.

The course of the exploring party from Pike
was northward, following the course of the
Mississippi.   Before reaching what is now
Quincy, they passed a night with two bachelors
from northern New York.   In his journal he
noted that these two young men would probably become permanent settlers, and had the
requisites of character to become good citizens,
a settlement having such a nucleus being, to
his mind, an important item in estimating the
value of the adjacent lands.   What sagacity
was manifested in that conclusion will be left
to those who for more than forty years have
known Governor John Wood and Willard
Keyes Esq., of Quincy, the young New Yorkers
of log-cabin remembrance.

Mr. Wood and your father arrived in Illinois
about the same time, Mr. Wood going north,
your father remaining at Edwardsville, though
they had not known of each other before the
meeting at the cabin.   Mr. Keyes went out
about the same time, but I think was a schoolmaster somewhere near the Wabash River
previous to joining Mr. Wood.[7]

[7] John Wood was a New Yorker who came to Illinois in early manhood in 1819.   In March, 1820, in

Towards the end of their exploration they happened upon the premises of Ossian M. Ross, who, with a sturdy wife, had just settled himself at what is now Lewistown, Fulton County.[8] The travelers arrived there in a company with Willard Keyes, he located a farm in Pike County about thirty-five miles southeast of Quincy. In 1821 he visited the site of Quincy and soon thereafter purchased a quarter section of land and erected the first building where the city now stands. Until his death in 1880, aside from temporary absences, Quincy remained the home of Governor Wood. During this period of almost sixty years he held numerous offices, local and state, the best known of these, perhaps, being the governorship of Illinois. His residence, a beautiful colonial mansion erected in 1835, is now the home of the Quincy Historical Society.

Willard Keyes was born on a Vermont farm in 1792. In 1817 he came west to Prairie du Chien in the party of Rev. Samuel Peters, who was seeking to secure confirmation to himself of the noted grant of Wisconsin land made to Jonathan Carver, the explorer, in 1767. Peters returned to the East in the spring of 1818, but Keyes remained at Prairie du Chien, conducting one of the first schools in Wisconsin. In the spring of 1819 he journeyed on a raft down river to Clarksville, Mo., where he lay sick for six months. Not long after this he entered the farming parnership with Governor Wood already noted. In the spring of 1824 he followed Wood to Quincy, and built the second house there. Until his death in 1872 he remained one of the leading citizens of the place. Mr. Keyes prospered financially, and with the proceeds of a bequest made by him Willard Hall was built by the Chicago Theological Seminary.

[8] Ossian M. Ross was a New Yorker who served in the War of 1812 and thereby acquired title to land

most hungry condition; their stock of crackers being spent they had lived on meat and water for a day or two. Ross received them very graciously, and the good wife set herself about preparing a meal for the hungry guests, which was supplied with abundance, and apparent good nature, though looking terribly aghast at the havoc made on her stores of honey, bacon, and corn-dodgers. I wonder if it then ever crossed her mind that one of her barefooted, smooth-faced hopefuls would ever figure as a representative in Congress, at Washington.

While on this survey, he encountered several other explorists, and it was amusing to hear of the raptures of some of them. One old gentleman—a good Methodist—followed the course of the Mississippi, and the farther north he advanced the more enthusiastic he became in admiration of the country, and when he arrived at the point where Quincy now is, and clambered to the top of the high mound that overlooked the noble river, his raptures knew no bounds, and throwing up his arms he exclaimed: "Glory, glory, glory!

in the Military Tract. He settled on it in 1821, and the town of Lewiston, named in honor of his son, Lewis Ross, was soon after laid out on a portion of it. Fulton County was organized in 1823, and Lewiston was made the county seat. Until 1829 Ross was the leading citizen of the new settlement. In that year he moved to Havana, becoming the first permanent settler of Mason County. Here he passed the remainder of his life.

I'm on the Mount! the Mount! I'm on the Mount of Glory!'' How would his righteous soul be vexed could he witness the demolition of his Mount Pisgah, through which is made the deep cut called Main Street? A young blade from New York or Philadelphia, after visiting the ''Bounty Tract,'' and crossing the Illinois River at Peoria Lake, went into ecstasies in describing the beauties of the scenery, and found, to his own surprise, that he was a poet, and declared that he could not leave without giving utterance to his feelings, not only because he had enjoyed so much, but that the sublimity should raise him to poetic transports, as an evidence of which he sent the following to his bachelor friends:

> "I am all in my glory when I think of Peoria,
>   That gentle and beautiful lake,
>   Where the goose and the swan do the waters
>   adorn,
>   There pleasure I mean for to take.
>
> With a wife by my side down the waters I'll
>   glide
>   With a love that shall banish all fear;
> And then we will roam to our cabin, our
>   home,
>   Nor dream that an Indian is near.''

I have forgotten the rest.

Towards the spring of 1821 Shurtleff, who had been a few months in the country, having fully decided to take to himself a wife, informed your father of the fact. He said he had had his pick of all the native girls, and had

decided on the "Squire's daughter, Polly."
He had popped the question, secured his
bird, but how about a cage? Would your
father let him bring his bride to the cabin
and she become housekeeper, and be their
boarder? Your father was willing, so Shurtleff
went to St. Louis, bought Polly a silk dress
and a straw bonnet and they were married,
and became host and hostess of the establishment. The bonnet and dress had a magic
influence on the mind of pretty Polly, as she
had never before worn anything that had not
been woven by her good mother, spun from
the cotton raised in their "patch," (garden),
and colored by indigo weed of their own
growing. The dress and bonnet were also a
subject of deep interest in the settlement.
Those who did not see her wear them "to
preaching," could yet have the benefit of calling at the cabin. Some thought Polly "too
much set up," but on the whole it was agreed
that she bore her honors meekly.

Poor Polly. In speaking of Polly I omitted
to say that she was a daughter of Esquire
Kilpatrick, familiarly called "Squire Davy,"
and as they were our nearest, and indeed our
most reliable neighbors among the "white
folks," we were brought into closer acquaintance than with any others. Perhaps I should
explain that "white folks" was a name given
in derision to the first emigrants from the western and southern states. An old Tennessee

woman who had a terrific opinion of the
Yankees, said: "I am getting skeery about them
'ere Yankees; there is such a power of them
coming in that they and the Injuns will squatch
out all the white folks." Nothing afterward
would exasperate them more than to have a
Yankee call them white folks.

When your father first went to look after
his farm he wanted a boarding place, and
"Squire Davy's" was recommended. He
and Wright accordingly took board there until their cabin was built, and Commodore
Yoakum had removed, thereby leaving his
cabin for their stable. The 'Squire had, I believe, been a schoolmaster in Barrens, Kentucky, the place from which they came. His
wife was naturally smart and industrious, the
latter qualification minus in " Squire Davy."
She could read, and entered into all the political
interests that came to her knowledge; kept
herself and family clean and comfortably clad.
She, with her daughters, Peggy and Polly,
had mauled rails enough to fence a "truck
patch," and a cotton and indigo patch. Here
every year she planted her cotton, indigo,
cabbage, potatoes, and whatever else the wants
and appetites of her family called for. The
whole family were clothed in the winter in
linsey and cotton, all of their own manufacture. During the summer a skirt with a waist
of copperas and blue plaid homespun, with a
necessary undergarment, constituted the dress

of the female portion of the family, with the exception of Mrs. Kilpatrick, who very wisely covered her neck with a kerchief made of the same material as their dresses. She was a short, broad, square-built woman, and the kerchief, a yard square, was none too ample to protect her well developed proportions.

I have been thus particular in my description that you may, in imagination, look at two handsome young gentlemen seated at the table with the 'Squire and lady, Peggy and Polly. Six was the number usually at log cabin tables, for the reason that six plates, one platter, six knives and forks, six tin cups — or, possibly among the more aristocratic, six cups and saucers — constituted the table outfit. On a little bench in the corner of the cabin stood the water bucket, with a gourd, for drinking. It was the custom for each one, after being satisfied with the solids at the table, to walk to the bucket and take their last course from the gourd. Then, while the younger scions were scrambling for what remained on the table, the older members of the family — both male and female — would seat themselves comfortably around the fire with each a pipe, showing their own inventive genius. Several varieties might be seen on such occasions, but the most common was a piece of corn-cob dug out for the bowl of the pipe, with an alder quill inserted for the stem.

Two such young men as our young bachelors

coming into the settlement, buying land, and actually going to work on their farms, created quite a sensation, and some looked with an evil eye on the 'Squire for taking the two Yankees into his family; some had always thought that "Old Davy was little better than a Yankee, anyhow." Some thought his wife had an eye for the future of her daughters; that Polly might do for Tillson, but as for Peggy it was decided she was too ugly even for a Yankee, although they were sure Mrs. Kilpatrick was for "hitching her to Wright." Jesse Buzan and Milton Shurtleff arriving settled that question, but the neighbors thought Davy and wife were "awful spited"—disappointed—at not getting Wright and Tillson.

Those who now go to the Far West can look forward to a rapid improvement, and with the facilities for traveling do not feel that where they have set themselves down is the place they must stay, or leave at a great sacrifice, and they can have but little idea of the discouragements the young adventurers of that country must have encountered. Nothing but a most indomitable perseverance could have caused them to remain, and I have felt like attributing to them a higher commendation than has yet been accorded to such. The new arrangement and change from bachelor housekeeping did not prove pleasant. Mine host showed his cloven foot in various ways. He quarreled with his wife's relations, and Mrs. Kilpatrick, after an encounter with her son-in-law, would report it to your father. While with them your father had a shake of the ague; knowing he had nothing to hope for there, in case of sickness, and feeling pretty sure, as the natives termed it, that he was "in for a smart grip of agy," he started at night and rode to Rev. Mr. Townsend's, seven miles towards Edwardsville, where he stayed to have another shake. The next being the intermediate day, he rode to Mr. Hoxie's, twenty-five miles farther, and waited over there for another shake, which Mrs. Hoxie said "beat all the shakes she ever saw; he shuck the hull cabin." The next day he went to Edwardsville, where he was kindly nursed and cared for by Mrs. Randall, the good old Methodist lady he had boarded with, and mother to Mr. Randall, the recorder. When he thought himself well enough he went over to Missouri, but the fatigue of the journey brought on a relapse. He was fortunate, however, in reaching his friend Hallet's.

In the spring of 1822 he rented his cabin to Mr. Rountree. Shurtleff, having entered land adjoining his farm, put up a cabin, where with his Polly he commenced—as he termed it— "on his own hook." Mr. Rountree was also putting up a cabin on his own land. Joel Wright built the same year on his quarter section, so there was quite a log-cabin neighborhood within a mile square. The cabins could be seen from each other in the winter, but in the summer the thick foliage and the high corn-fields shut out all intrusion from prying neighbors, and equally all sense of human companionship, making at times the truth of Alexander Selkirk's lines, ''I am monarch of all I survey,'' &c., more forcible than poetic.

In April your father and Mr. Augustus Collins started together on horseback, one for Connecticut, the other for Massachusetts, both on the same errand. Mr. Collins married a Miss Sanders — she is now the wife of Dr. Gillett, of Jacksonville, Illinois. It was the plan that we should all return in company to Illinois, but your father being detained by business we did not start until a week later, and it became one of the occupations of our journey to study the hotel registers, looking for the record of their family. Besides Augustus Collins and wife, were his father and mother, his sisters, Miss Eliza, Miss Almira (since Mrs. Giddings), and Maria, the youngest, a beautiful and accomplished young lady, who died not long after their arrival; four brothers, Anson, Michael, William, and Frederic, the last the only surviving one.

After reaching Illinois we kept up as much of an acquaintance as the distance of our location would admit, your father and Mr. Collins always retaining their kind feeling toward each other, and the friendship commencing so early has always been cherished by me, and I have ever felt a warm attachment for that family, and have regretted that I did not more frequently see Mrs. Giddings after her coming to Quincy. It was in the summer of 1825 that we made our first visit to the Collins family. We met there Mr. Giddings, who, as I afterwards found, was looking among the eastern ladies for a better half, and the result was his marriage the next year to Miss Almira Collins. I did not again see Mrs. Giddings until after the birth of Frederic, in the autumn of 1827. At that time Augustus Collins, with his brother Anson, had commenced business in St. Louis, leaving his father and mother in Unionville (now Collinsville). William Collins had married, and occupied the old mansion, and with his brothers was engaged in the flour business, and running a distillery. The latter, though a business of much profit, they gave up for conscience sake. When the Collins family, father and sons, decided to give up distilling, the old lady would not consent to have the still sold, but had it bruised and so demolished that it could only be sold for old copper. She said "no more sin and misery should come from that still."

OUR JOURNEY

In 1822 it was still a great event to undertake a journey to Illinois, and many were the direful remarks and conclusions about my going. Your grandmother dreaded my starting without any lady companion, and was much relieved to find that a Mrs. Cushman, a widow lady, whose husband had been a lawyer in Halifax, and who had but one child — a son, settled near Cincinnati — was waiting an opportunity to go and end her days with her beloved Joshua, and that your father had offered her a seat in our carriage, which offer had been accepted. Your uncle Robert was also to go. The carriage had been built at Bedford, Massachusetts, under your father's directions, expressly for the journey. Your Great-grandmother Briggs had seen the carriage pass her house, and in telling how she felt at parting with her eldest granddaughter, and the sadness it had given her to see the carriage that was to take me away, was not aware that she said "hearse" instead of carriage. It amused those who heard it, but they had too much reverence for her feelings to tell her of the mistake.

How hard it is to shake off the sadness of our young days. Partings, the breaking up of families and home attachments, have always been to me particularly painful, and the sad forebodings I was constantly hearing at that time of the fearful journey, and the dismal

31

backwoods life which awaited me were not calculated to dispel the clouds that would sometimes come over me. I did not know then, as I realize now, that I was more ready to be influenced by fears than by hopes. My timidity through life has been my infirmity, want of self-confidence and a shrinking from notoriety marked my early life; and it is only from a sense of duty to myself and children that I have, in a measure, overcome the folly that has kept me back from many good performances.

I did not intend to enter into an investigation of my own particular temper and disposition, but found myself — before I was aware of it — doling out my shortcomings. It has been my misfortune to dwell on my own weakness.

* * * * * * *

We left my father's house at Kingston, October 6, 1822.[9] Our carriage being some-

[9] Mrs. Tillson's narrative of her journey from Massachusetts to Illinois may profitably be compared with O. M. Spencer's account of a similar journey taken by his parents a third of a century earlier, published in the volume of the Lakeside Classics series for 1917 (*The Indian Captivity of O. M. Spencer 3–12*). The Spencers journeyed by the Forbes Road, later known as the Pennsylvania Road, across Pennsylvania to a tributary of the Ohio, traveling thence by water to Cincinnati. The Tillsons, setting out from Plymouth County, Massachusetts, followed in general the shore line to New York city. From here they crossed New Jersey to Philadelphia and thence made

what such a vehicle as we would now call a two seated buggy, at that time the name buggy was not known. The seats were so made that a trunk could be fitted under each one of them, and there was room in front for a bonnet trunk that held my leghorn bonnet, and a portmanteau containing the gentlemen's change of clothing. Mrs. Cushman's trunk rode behind, and with a little bamboo basket containing my night clothes, brushes, &c., and a lunch basket, we found ourselves pretty closely packed.

their way southwesterly to Cumberland, Maryland, which was the eastern terminus of the great National Road. Construction of this had been begun in 1811, and by 1818 had been carried to Wheeling on the Ohio at an average cost per mile of $13,000. In later years the National Road was carried westward across central Ohio and Indiana, with St. Louis as its ultimate goal. The latter point was never reached, however, the development of other routes and methods of transportation causing the discontinuance of the project. Over this great highway poured a flood of traffic, both passenger and freight, and the National Road was one of the important agencies in the development of the West. From Wheeling the Tillsons followed Zane's Trace through Zanesville and Lancaster to Chillicothe. As far as Zanesville this was later the route of the National Road when in 1825 construction westward from Wheeling was begun. The National Road continued due westward to Columbus and Indianapolis, while Zane's Trace turned southwestwardly to Maysville on the Ohio, whence the highway continued to Lexington in Kentucky. At some point between Chillicothe and Maysville the Tillsons turned westward to Williamsburg (in eastern Clermont County) and thence to Cincinnati.

A Woman's Story

We were to travel at about the rate of one hundred miles in three days, and St. Paul-like, commenced our journey coast-wise. We passed through Providence, stopping to dine with Seth Allen, who had formerly been a neighbor of your Grandfather Tillson's. I speak of this because theirs were the last faces I saw of those I had known before, and not until four years after, when your Uncle Charles arrived in Illinois, did I see any face that I had before looked upon after leaving the Allens' on my second day from home. Our course carried us along the southern, the shore line of Connecticut, passing through New Haven. We arrived at New York in eight days. It being my first visit, I was much disappointed to find the city almost depopulated by the yellow fever.[10] We knew before starting that the fever was prevailing to some extent; but as intelligence did not then, as now, go with lightning speed, and we had been so long on the way, the extent of the sickness was not known to us. We rode into New York in the morning, but it had a very desolate appearance. The inhabitants had closed their places of business,

[10] William Newnham Blane, a portion of whose *Excursion through the United States and Canada during the Years 1822–1823* was reprinted in *Pictures of Illinois One Hundred Years Ago*, the preceding volume in the Lakeside Classics, was in New York at the same time as Mrs. Tillson, and in his book of travels gives a vivid picture of the conditions there during the yellow fever epidemic.

and the merchants had removed their goods out of what was then termed the city. The place where Union Square now is, was country, and those who were willing to risk the chances of yellow fever so near them had erected shanties and were displaying their goods. There was a large brick building where an Irishman kept a decent tavern. They were holding a political caucus the night we stopped there.

At Philadelphia we stayed a day, putting up at a Quaker boarding house. We went out and bought a white merino shawl and some winter trimmings for my large leghorn bonnet. We did not then change as often as now, having a winter, spring, summer, and fall bonnet. Those who had a nice leghorn, as was mine, changed the trimmings with the season. Those who could afford it wore ostrich feathers in the winter, while in the summer flowers were substituted. Feathers at that time were thought to be in bad taste for summer wear. I enjoyed my day in Philadelphia; also my whole journey through New Jersey and Pennsylvania. The country was very different from anything I had seen. Having been brought up on the sandy soil of the old Colony, among the pine woods, where every farmer is a poor man, and those who have farms and are rich have made themselves so by manufacture or commerce, it seemed strange to see the big Dutch barns, which in the distance we continually mistook for churches. The inhabitants also interested me. We stopped every night, and between Philadelphia and Lancaster found ourselves in houses where they could not speak a word of English, and our pantomime performances were sometimes very amusing. I can now recall some things which occurred while your father and I were trying to come to some understanding with the host and hostess. I can now see your Uncle Robert in his mulberry suit, both arms hanging straight from his shoulders, not speaking or moving himself, but good-naturedly watching the movements of the rest.

Arrived at Wheeling we stopped for break-fast, and then in a ferry boat crossed the Ohio, where I was somewhat disappointed. The river was very low at that time, and its narrow stream between two sandy shores I looked on with other eyes and other emotions than I had in store for the ''beautiful Ohio.'' From Wheeling we went across the country to Williamsburgh, a town twenty miles from Cincinnati, where we were to leave Mrs. Cushman with her son. I should like to describe Mrs. Cushman, but now feel like plodding my way through Ohio. After crossing the Ohio River, a new scene opened to me, and my initiation to a new country began. From Cumberland, Pennsylvania, to Wheeling, we had traveled on the National Road, but it extended no farther, and after that we were left to make our way as best we could over such roads as Ohio at that

time could offer. When we were wading
through swampy, boggy bottom lands we hailed
a corduroy with joy, not that corduroys were our
particular fancy, but anything for a variety;
and when the jostling, jolting, up and down
process became unbearable, a change to a mud
hole was quite soothing.[11] We were not all the
time, however, in so sad an extremity. We
sometimes for hours would ride through high
and dry woodlands where there had been roads
surveyed and the under-growth cleared out the
width of a carriage road, and every few rods
we would find what they termed a blaze, which
was a tree with the bark hacked off, and these
served as guide boards.

At Zanesville we found the first comfortable
stopping place after leaving Wheeling. We
went from there to Chillicothe, where we found
a good house. This place always recalls Mrs.
Cushman. She found in the morning that in
passing to her bedroom the night before she
had come in contact with fresh paint, and had
marred the appearance of her nice blue cloth
traveling suit. She went to the painter, showed

[11] A corduroy road was made over wet or swampy
places by the simple process of throwing down logs
at right angles to the line of travel to constitute a
roadbed. Of course the logs would be of varying
dimensions and would sink varying distances into the
mud or swamp, or at times become displaced altogether, thus affording to those who traveled over
them in wheeled vehicles an ever constant element
of change and surprise.

him her garment, and asked for some spirits of turpentine. The painter looked indifferent, and told her he had no turpentine, whereupon she grew earnest, and asked him what kind of a painter he could be, not to have spirits of turpentine, to which he gave her some rather waggish answer. She then drew his attention to the intrinsic worth of the garment, by telling him she paid so many dollars per yard in Boston, where she had had it made just before starting on her journey. Nothing moved by her sorrows, he kept at his work, being very respectful, though looking wonderfully amused. Mrs. Cushman, finding she could accomplish nothing with the painter, resorted to mine host, who, with his wife, two or three greasy girls from the kitchen, and all the younglings of the family, were open-mouthed, listening to her sad story. A happy thought at last moved some brain of the group to go to the druggist's and obtain the desired remedy, which, after much ado and hard rubbing, finally produced the erasive effect desired, so that our friend went on her journey as well satisfied as if nothing had happened.

Mrs. Cushman was not a fault-finding woman, and with a few outbreaks like the one named excepted, made a pleasant companion, and accommodated herself to the inconveniences of such a journey better than most people would have done. She was a fine looking woman, always neat and well dressed, and had in her young days been called a beauty; was a sister of Thomas Hubbard of Hanson, the rich man of the town; had married Jotham Cushman of Halifax, an educated and handsome man, brother to Joshua Cushman of Maine. After her husband's death her house was given up and she left minus house, home, and every means of support, and entirely dependent on her brother's bounty. Her only son, Joshua, had gone to Ohio to seek his fortune; had married, and his wife had died, leaving one child. Her desire to be with her son and to take charge of his little daughter made her prefer the uncertainty of a new western home to the comfortable provision her brother had extended to her in his own family.

On inquiring for Williamsburgh, after leaving Chillicothe, we could find no one who knew of such a place. At last a shrewd backwoodsman where we spent the night told us it was only a "stake town." It had been staked out but they had not made any "improvements" yet; he reckoned they might get up some cabins in the spring. Did not know any man by the name of Cushman. There were a few families settled in the timber, near where the town was staked off; shouldn't wonder if the man might be there; seems like he had heard the name. Poor Mrs. Cushman! I hardly dared look at her. How could she bear the change? I felt sad, sad indeed. Not so with Mrs. Cushman; the thought of being so near her only child seemed to exclude every other feeling. The weariness from her long journey, the racking from the corduroy roads; and even the few remaining spots of white lead that had clung to her blue skirt, were all forgotten in the thought that in a few hours she might meet her Joshua. Such is a mother's love. A father may love his children dearly, tenderly, a husband a wife, a wife a husband, a brother a sister, a sister a brother, but none of those can comprehend a mother's love.

It was Saturday, about noon, when we arrived at the house of Mr. Jernegan; the Buckeyes called him "Johnnygins." The family were from Nantucket. A sea-faring man had been Mr. Jernegan. He had moved to Ohio, and a pretty daughter of his had married Mr. Joshua Cushman, a handsome young Yankee. We found Mr. Cushman and child—a sweet little girl, about three years old—at Mr. Jernegan's. The family were living in a small brick building that had been put up with the intention of putting a large front to what they designed for a kitchen, but at the time of our visit it served for kitchen, dining-room, and parlor, and two little bedrooms partitioned from the kitchen completed the mansion. Mrs. Jernegan, a plain, sensible, modest woman, who, with her daughter, did the work of the family, received Mrs. Cushman politely, but seeing her looking at the stately appearance of Mrs. Cushman, and then at her own accomodations—her little bedrooms and plain kitchen arrangements—I could see and understand the "Oh, dear! what I am to do?" although unuttered. We were, however, relieved when Joshua pointed out a small brick building which he said he could make ready and go to housekeeping in a short time. We made the best possible time after leaving Mrs. Cushman on Saturday, for Cincinnati, where we arrived Sunday morning in time for church, but in no plight for church-going. We stopped at a house kept by a Mr. Fox.

I forgot to mention a night we spent between Wheeling and Cincinnati with a Bostonian. We were told through the day, when, as was our custom, we inquired for a stopping-place for the next night, that there was no tavern on the road, but that by turning a little off the "big road," we would find "a Yankee man that had settled in, and had made a clearing, and sometimes kept public." We reached the cabin about sunset and found a little man who, with his big wife, decided that we could stay. The little man seemed to be a Massachusetts Yankee, out-and-out, but his bigger half I could not understand her. She did not seem to work, or to know how; did not look too good to work, or to know enough to be a lady. Another woman seemed to be housekeeper and cook. The little man had a neighbor with him helping him to kill sheep. We made no protest against the slaughter, for one of the most

urgent demands of our nature was in full
force, we having eaten nothing since breakfast,
and the savory odors made us almost rebellious at the tardiness of the cook, but the whiskey
bottle with which our host and his neighbor
were exhilarating themselves did not suit me.
They prepared a mug of whiskey toddy for Mrs.
Cushman and myself, but both said "No;
thank you;" hostess didn't thank, but said
"Yes." After supper, on a bureau which stood
in the room, I found a number of Massachusetts
papers and a file of the Boston *Recorder*.
While I was trying to reconcile the paper with
the whiskey, the little man handed me a late
number of the *Recorder*, saying that his son
was the editor, and sent him the paper every
week. I said, "Nathaniel Willis edits the *Recorder*." He said, "Yes, Nat.; I gave Nat.
my trade; I was a printer. Nat. has got along
pretty well; Nat. is the editor now." "Then
you are the father of Nathaniel Willis?"
"Yes; I worked at printing until I got tired,
and thought I would give it up to Nat. and
come west and try farming: pretty rough yet;
but I got tired of the printing office."[12]

[12] Nathaniel Willis, born in 1780 and died in 1870,
was a prominent New England editor of his day. In
1803 he established the Portland *Eastern Argus;* in
1816 he founded the Boston *Recorder*, one of the
earliest religious newspapers in the world. In 1827
he founded the *Youth's Companion*, which is said to
have been the first children's paper ever published.
The father, whom the Tillsons encountered in Ohio,

Some twelve or fifteen years afterward I met N. P. Willis at the American Hotel in New York. He had just returned from Europe with his English wife, and they were showing off, to the amusement of other guests of the house. I thought then how much easier his grand-dad might have dropped on his knee and laced the shoes of his big half than could N. P. with his tight unmentionables all strapped down; to accomplish which gallant act gracefully under the circumstances, required some skill. In after years I became acquainted with Richard Willis, who told me that the wife I saw was not his grandmother, but that she was a Virginian, and I then comprehended her— evidently "poor white folks." When the fastidious N. P. Willis went through the West, and was shocked at the rudeness of Quincy and the Quincy House, I again thought of the old grand-dad. Fanny Fern, had she known of it, might have written a book about "The days of my grand-dad; the jolliest man that ever broke bread."

At Cincinnati a serious question arose; the possibility of getting through Indiana with a carriage seemed doubtful. There had been a continuous rain during our travel through Ohio,

had been editor and proprietor successively of several papers before coming west. N. P. Willis, son of the founder of *Youth's Companion*, was a well-known poet and literary worker of the first half of the nineteenth century.

and the river, which at Wheeling appeared so insignificant, had expanded itself into magnificence at Cincinnati, and when they talked about the streams in Indiana not being fordable in consequence of the late rains I, for the first time, received the idea as a reality that there was such a thing as an inhabited country without bridges — my education was just beginning. After much talking and due deliberation it was decided that we should put our carriage and all our baggage on board a little steamboat bound for Louisville; that your father and myself were to go on board as passengers while your Uncle Robert was to proceed on horseback, riding one horse and leading the other, as it was possible for a horseman to head the creeks and pass where there was no carriage road. It was my first steamboat experience, and I had at least a quiet time, I being the only lady passenger. The little boat was new and clean; a small cabin separated from the main cabin and containing four berths were the accomodations intended for lady passengers, and we had this to ourselves. We were on the boat several days. After a day or two a gentleman came in and commenced an acquaintance with us, introducing himself as Mr. Dent, from Missouri. He said he had wanted to say to me that there would be no impropriety or discomfort in my occupying a seat by the stove in the gentleman's cabin; that as the ladies' cabin had been painted while at Cincinnati, it was unsafe to remain in it; and suggested our keeping it open and exposed to the air through the day. He said that his father came to his death in consequence of occupying a newly painted apartment. It was a very kind suggestion and I have always remembered it, and when his daughter married Ulysses, and Ulysses became our President, and when I hear Mrs. Grant spoken of with respect, I always feel well pleased, and remember the benevolence that characterized her father.

When we arrived at Louisville I was kindly received by two families of your father's cousins. Mr. Joseph Danforth and Mr. Edmund Lewis had both, with their families, resided there four or five years, and were partners in the drygoods business. Mr. Danforth had a family of four children, Mr. Lewis, a son. The year following Mr. and Mrs. Danforth lost two of their daughters, leaving them Joseph and Julia, who are still living. Mrs. Danforth and Mr. Lewis were own cousins to your father. At Louisville we found our prospects no better in regard to getting through the country in a carriage, and after staying there several days — as a boat was about to leave for New Orleans, probably the last one for several weeks — we decided to take passage for Shawneetown. Your Uncle Robert had not arrived with the horses, and as he was inexperienced in travel we felt much solicitude on his account, but it seemed our only alternative.

We landed at Shawneetown early Monday morning; had expected to arrive there the Saturday previous. We had a poor apology for a boat, and accomodations were only known by name. Captain Dent, who was also a passenger, decided to keep by the boat in hopes of finding a New Orleans boat at the mouth of the Ohio that would take him to St. Louis. He said a great deal to us about the presumption of trying to cross Illinois by carriage, and thought we had better even go to New Orleans if we failed to meet a boat at Cairo, but your father seemed very hopeful, and besides we both felt as if we could go no farther until we had heard from Robert, from whom we had parted at Cincinnati, and had heard nothing for nearly two weeks. Mr. Dent in parting gave me a fatherly grip of the hand, with an assurance that he should feel interested in knowing that I was safely through all the bogs and bayous and corduroys that I might encounter. The swimming creeks and miry bottoms were all Greek to me, and his look so mysterious that I did not understand. I was able to interpret it before the end of my journey.

We walked from the boat landing to the hotel, a short distance, but it was raining hard and the mud was deep and adhesive, and I reached the house very much fatigued. It was before breakfast, and after getting me to the bar-room fire — the only one that never went out in the house — your father went to

look after the "plunder," a western term for
baggage. When he returned he thought I had
better take some whiskey to ward off the effects
of the morning's exposure. It was the first
time I had ever tasted it and though always an
impalatable beverage to me, I shall never forget how disgusted and outraged I was by that
first taste at Shawneetown.[13] Our hotel — the
only brick house in the place — made quite
a commanding appearance from the river,
towering, as it did, among the twenty — more
or less — log cabins and the three or four box-
looking frames. One or two of these were
occupied as stores, one was a doctor's office;
a lawyer's shingle graced the corner of one,
cakes and beer another.

The hotel lost its significance, however, on
entering its doors. The finish was of the
cheapest kind, the plastering hanging loose
from the walls, the floors carpetless, except
with nature's carpeting; with that they were
richly carpeted. The landlord — a poor white
man from the South — was a whiskey keg in the
morning, and a keg of whiskey at night; stupid
and gruff in the morning, by noon could talk
politics and abuse the Yankees, and by sundown
was brave for a fight. His wife kept herself
in the kitchen; his daughters — one married

[13] Shawneetown was at this time one of the two
principal towns of Illinois, the other being Kaskaskia;
the former was the land office for southeastern Illinois and the principal center for its travel and traffic.

and two single — performed the agreeable to strangers; the son-in-law, putting on the airs of a gentleman, presided at the table, carving the pork, dishing out the cabbage, and talking big about his political friends. His wife — being his wife — he seemed to regard as a notch above the other branches of the family, and had her at his right hand at the table, where she sat with her long curls, and with her baby in her lap. Baby always seemed to be hungry while mammy was eating her dinner, and so "little honey" took dinner at the same time. Baby didn't have any table-cloth — new manners to me. Your father's caution was always at hand, to try not to give them the impression that I was proud, with an allusion to the prejudice felt by this class of people toward the Yankees. We had a room fronting the street and could see everyone that came to the ferry, which was directly opposite the house, and my occupation from Monday until Friday was watching for Robert and the horses. We not only were in great haste to get away from such a disagreeable place, but were anxious for the safety of Robert, who had never before been left to do for himself. Indeed, we were all inexperienced and untried.

I can now recall the joy I felt when late in the afternoon on Friday, your father and Uncle Robert presented themselves before the hotel. Your father had crossed the ferry several times each day, hoping to meet the long-looked-for;

it availed nothing, but for the want of something else to do, and to quiet his anxiety, he kept on the move. Robert had sold one of the horses, finding it tiresome and difficult to lead one while he rode another, but had retained the best horse, "Charley." The first thing to be done was to buy a horse. Our landlord was quite at his ease as a horse-jockey, and early the next morning there appeared an array of men with their horses, each hoping to get a good bargain out of the green Yankees. After a few hours bantering it was decided that we were to have a little black pony, strangely contrasting with the noble bearing of our "Charley" horse.

Our landlord was very officious through it all, and finally closed up his morning's task by having a fight with one of the countrymen. I was at the open window and witnessed the whole disgraceful outbreak. I had often before heard of the western gouging and fighting, but never before saw a fight, and hope I never may again. I can now see the landlord, thin, tall, and erect, with his gray locks floating in the air, using the most unheard of profanity, "clinched," as they termed it, with a fat, squatty-looking beast of a being, each aiming at the other's eyes, and each showing that their dodging powers had been well trained. The desire of an ignorant westerner to stand up for his "rights," as he called them, was the predominant feeling of his nature, and when these rights were encroached upon he knew no other redress than by strength of muscle; so when the countryman called the landlord ''a pint-blank, mean liar,'' because he had not sold his horse to the Yankee, it was exasperating, but when the countryman saw your father counting out the bright ''shiners'' to one of his neighbors—the former owner of our pony— his wrath knew no bounds. He abused Hilton, who would not take abuse, hence the fight. Some half dozen of the lookers-on separated them, and old Hilton, after mopping his face with his shirt-sleeve, went into the house.

We then busied ourselves in getting ready to start as soon as possible, and I went to dinner light-hearted at the thought of its being the last meal at that place. Old Boniface didn't appear at dinner, and after going through the form I went to my room to put on my outer gear for the journey. I was standing with my back towards the door when I heard a voice behind me, and, looking around, there stood Hilton, with his face covered with plasters. It was always my weakness to scream when suddenly startled, so I perpetrated one of the most unearthly yells—which your father had not yet become acquainted with. He was coming to the room, and was near the door when the explosion took place. I do not know which one of the two was most puzzled to know what ailed me. As the landlord had only come to the room for the trunks, and we were hurrying to get away, not much explanation was necessary.

It was not in accordance with my ideas to start on a journey on Saturday afternoon, but the thing had been talked over and the chances for Sabbath observance seemed less here than to launch out into one of the broad prairies. We thought perhaps we might come to some more congenial place; at least we should be relieved from the drunkenness and profanity for which Shawneetown was at that time noted; so about two o'clock we rode out of Shawneetown.

Before leaving, your father met a Mr. McClintock, who gave him a way-bill of the country through which we were to pass, with the names of the best places for meals and lodging. Mr. McClintock was a government surveyor, and had been all over the country, and we found it a great assistance to have his directions. The first place found on our bill was Brice Hanna's, where we could find good accomodations for man and beast. I well remember the joyous freedom we realized after leaving Shawneetown. All were relieved from the anxiety caused by our separation, and were again at liberty to pursue our journey, and as it was my first introduction to the State which was to be my home I tried to make the dismal-looking bottom prairie through which we were passing look cheerful and homelike, merely because it was Illinois. Your father suggested that we should not make up our minds yet as to the beauty of a western prairie from what we saw of the "bottom lands," and as I could not succeed in finding anything to admire in the prospect around, I was willing to let the future take care of itself, and for variety started a song. The gentlemen were both singers, and I, putting in what power I possessed, we made the woods and prairies resound.

After riding about two hours we came to a horrible corduroy, and were relieved when that came to an end and we found ourselves at a running brook, where we stopped to give our horses water. After giving them due time to slake their thirst, and the signal was given them to move on, we found them a fixture, and all the coaxing and whipping that was alternately administered had no effect to produce a forward movement. As "Charley" had always been so reliable, never having departed from his lofty bearing, the conclusion was that the new horse must be at fault, consequently a sound whipping was administered upon the poor darkey, who by plunging and trying to leap forward showed his willingness to obey. It then became evident that the trouble was with "Charley," who, when he was whipped, only floundered about in the water, and then settled himself down again. Your father looked perplexed and troubled, and on closer examination discovered the stump of an old tree at the bottom of the water which he thought might be the

cause of the difficulty. There being but one
way to get out of it, he commenced another
lashing of poor "Charley." I felt like crying
and I am not sure but that I gave myself up to
that indulgence. Your father seemed to feel
every lash that he administered to his poor
victim, who, finally, with one desperate leap
freed himself from his anchorage, and it was
found that one of his feet had been caught between two prongs of the stump, thereby holding
him fast. Joy came to us all when we found
that although "Charley" came out with a ragged
hoof and looking decidedly used up, he was
able to walk and to take us on our journey.
Your father had made up his mind — so he
told us afterwards — that one of his legs was
broken, and that he should be obliged to kill
him, and leave poor "Charley" by the wayside,
which would have been a most grievous thing
to him. He had purchased him before going
east with Mr. Collins in the spring; had rode
from Illinois to Massachusetts on horseback,
and then had driven him back to Illinois; and
he was such a rare specimen of all that was
reliable and elegant his loss would have been
to us irreparable.

After the excitement was over — the carriage
having been disengaged from the horses and
drawn back on the corduroy — finding it would
be some time before all could be in readiness
to move again, I discovered myself not in high
heart; that my enthusiasm for western prairies

was vanishing; that I was approaching the extreme of what Captain Artus afterwards called "gaudiloupiness." So I concluded as my only resource to start off on a brisk walk, expecting the carriage would soon overtake me, but after losing sight of my companions, and looking about into the swampy surroundings, things looked dubious and the dismals were getting a good hold of my feelings when I heard a most unearthly yell coming through the forest, and the vivid recollection of a panther story I had heard not long before coming to my help, I turned back and with a quicker step than I could take now hastened towards the carriage, not knowing whether I was going from or approaching the dreaded foe. I had heard that their manner of attack was to perch themselves on the branch of a tree, and when within reaching distance pounce upon their prey. Every rustling of the branches assured me that a panther was on the watch for me with a hungry appetite.

At last I reached the brook, where a new difficulty was presenting itself. The horses had become so thoroughly frightened that no urging or driving could get them near enough to hitch to the carriage, and while trying to invent some way to draw it over two teamsters came along, each having a large Pennsylvania wagon drawn by four horses. One of the forward horses — which they called the leader — had a saddle on, on which sat the owner of the team, one of the men looking as lordly as if he was leading an army to battle. Your father asked them if they would take off their forward horses and draw out the carriage. The man nearest — the lordly looking one — said he would do it for a "dorller." Your father not pretending to hear him, went on trying his own horses. The man again called out: "Stranger, I say, I'll do it for a dorller." Your father told him he was in difficulty and would be much obliged to anyone who would help him. The wagoner looked sulky, and the man in the rear wagon called out: "See here, Brice, you move along; it isn't me that leaves a stranger in a fix like this;" so the "dollar" man moved on and the other drove up, unhitched his horses, and putting them to our carriage drew it out of the water. The whole performance did not occupy ten minutes. When the man was on his horse again and ready for a start, your father bestowed many thanks on him, and we were soon on our way. We soon overtook the teams and inquired how far it was to Brice Hanna's, and were answered by the man who had helped us. We also asked if it was a good place to stop. Imagine our surprise when he pointed to the other man and said, "That is Brice Hanna." Brice pretended not to hear.

* * * * * * *

Old rheumatism took me by the hand a few weeks ago, and has held his grip so tightly

that I thought my pencilings were at an end;
but, having a release from my bondage, and
feeling quite lonely, I have concluded to resume
my recollections of western life. In recording
reminiscences of the past I have tried to give
a truthful description of events as they occurred forty-eight years ago. I probably have
forgotten many things that were, at the time
of their occurrence, interesting to me. I re-
gret that I have not the power within me to
give a more high-toned record, but as that
gift is not, and the subject not a soul-inspiring
one, I must be content to suit my story to the
log cabin surroundings, which are not wont to
elevate.

Mr. Hardy, a Presbyterian minister, who
used to have his home with us when in our
vicinity, said that on his first going west,
when he attempted to write he would find
himself falling into log cabin dialect, and log
cabin notions of things, and that he used to
get a volume of Burns' poems—of which
he was fond—and read, and then look at
the log walls of the cabin, then read again,
and look at his puncheon floor, and try to look
at them with a mind elevated by the inspiration
of reading, and he felt he had accomplished
quite an improved standard. But no such
experiment came to my help. The indescribable care devolving upon a housekeeper in
that new and rough country and the ways and
means to which one must resort in order to

keep up a comfortable establishment absorbed not only the physical strength of a Yankee housewife, but all the faculties of the mind had to be brought into requisition in order to secure a comfortable living.

I believe when I left off writing we were on our way to our night's station, and had been introduced to our host. I so vividly remember the events of that night that I will try to give you some idea of it. Brice Hanna was a tall, well-formed man with good features, and but for his surly expression might have been called handsome. When we arrived at his house he dismounted, came up to the carriage, and told us there was another house on the other side of the swamp where we could stay; that he had been from home all the week; that his wife was sick, and that we could not be accommodated *anyhow*. Your father told him that it was nearly sunset, and that he should not attempt to go through a five-mile swamp until he could do it by daylight, so we unpacked ourselves and moved towards the house, and with much fear and trembling I set my foot on the threshold of Brice Hanna's cabin. There was but one room in the main cabin, which I at once perceived was unusually clean for an establishment of that kind. There were two beds nicely made, with clean pillows and handsome bed-quilts, the floor clean, and the coarse chairs looking as if they had just been scrubbed. In a large, open fire-place was a cheerful fire of oak logs, which were supported by one old iron andiron and a stone on the other side. But what most puzzled me was a pretty woman — who did not seem to be more than twenty — sitting with her feet on a chair, and with pillows around her, and holding her infant in her lap. Her skin was very fair, and she had an abundance of jet black, curly hair, and bright, black eyes. She had on a pretty pink calico dress, which with her baby's gear had the appearance of thorough cleanliness. She looked a little annoyed when we first went in, but politely asked us to be seated, and by her manner we concluded that she was mistress of the mansion.

Brice had not made his appearance, but he finally came in bringing a stone, which he threw down with an oath, saying he had had his eye on that rock for some time, and thought it would be a match for the one in the fire-place. He commenced pulling out the andiron, swearing at the fire for being too hot. His wife looked on tremblingly, and asked why he was not willing to have the andiron remain, as it was "a heap handier than the stone." With another string of oaths he jerked out the poor andiron, and taking it to the door he threw it as far as he could into the yard. Such things might do for the broadcloth gentry, but he did not belong to the gentry; at the same time giving one of his menacing glances at us. He went out, but returned in a few minutes to say

to his wife that the woman she had there —
who, with her husband and boy, occupied a
little cabin in the yard — "should not stay in
his diggings another night," and with another
oath said, "clare them out." "Well, what is
the matter?" asked the trembling wife. "Matter! why the cursed —— " a list of epithets too
fearful to repeat; "infernal fool has let the hogs
and cows get into my corn-field and destroy
more corn and potatoes than thar eternally
cursed necks are worth; so I'll clare them
out," finishing off his sentence with another
string of oaths not to be outdone by Sancho
Panza's proverbs.

The poor wife would shrink down when the
blast was heaviest, but after he had gone would
brighten up again. When one of the storms had
subsided and he had gone out to anathematize
the man and boy with curses loud and heavy,
I ventured to ask her how long she had been a
cripple. She said only a few months; that just
before her baby was born she fell into the well
and broke some of her bones, and was so hurt
all over that she had not been able to walk since,
and if it had been God's will she should have
wished never to have come out alive. She was
ignorant, but pretty, and with a sweet expression; so much truthfulness was manifested in
all she said that my heart went out to her with
a compassion that I cannot express.

After awhile the fiend again made his appearance with a large slice of bacon and corn

bread in his hand, and with his foot he kicked along a chair until he reached his wife, and seating himself by her side he took out a long bowie knife and commenced eating. Looking at her with something of a subdued tone, he said: "This is the first corn bread and bacon I have tasted since I went from here." "Too bad," she remarked, pleasantly; "and what did you eat all the week?" "Why, you see, I was hauling for Marshall; Marshall is building a big house; and I have been hauling brick and timber. When I gits to the house Marshall will call to that infernal old black cook of his'n to get my supper, and the ——" usual list of expletives, "fool goes and makes me some coffee as black as her derned old face, and some of them 'are cussed light Yankee biscuits, and some beef that was just warmed through as the old bull was when he was running alive and bellering, and when you put your knife inter hit by thunder the blood would run. Haven't had a bite of pone, or corn-dodger, or hog meat, not any since last Monday morning." "Too bad; didn't they give you any milk?" "Jest so; axed for milk, and the old black devil brought me some jest from the cow; haven't seen a sip of buttermilk or clabber." "Too bad." She looked pleased that he had become sufficiently subdued to bear soothing.

We had previously called for supper, and were summoned into the cabin in the yard, which was used for a kitchen and dining-room.

The woman of all work — the wife of the man who didn't keep the hogs out of the cornfield — was standing at a side table where we were to be seated for our evening repast. I have forgotten what we had for food, but remember the cleanliness of the rough furnishing, and that a saucer standing on the table, filled with lard, with a strip of white cloth laid in it and one end raised up at the side of the saucer, burning, served to light the table and the whole room. We went back from our supper to where the happy pair were still seated, he looking as if he had blown another blast and had settled down to sulk, and the wife trying to look happy, and smiling through her tears. He sat awhile as if trying to think of something disagreeable to say or do. All at once a happy thought seemed to occur to him, and looking at us with malicious satisfaction he commenced a furious rubbing and scratching, pushing up his sleeves and looking at his wrists. He turned suddenly around and asked us if we had any beds of our own to stretch on for the night. He had seen all we took from the carriage, and knew that we had no beds along, and looked satanically happy when he announced that we would all get the itch, as all in the house had it, and swore that the cursed old fellow who couldn't keep the cows out of the corn-field had brought the itch to them. Such startling information would have been fearful had I not looked at the honest face of the poor wife, who, without uttering a word, showed plainly that it was news to her, and I felt sure it was only a scheme of his own to make us uncomfortable. He seemed disappointed that he had not made a greater sensation, and as no one replied to his last effort he settled himself to think of something else disagreeable.

At last, with a more extended swear than before, he said he was tired, and was going to bed; it would do for gentry, who could stay in bed as long as they pleased, to sit up late, "but I'm no gentry, and I'm going to bed." There were two beds in the room, standing foot to foot, on the side opposite the fire-place. One was for us, the other for Brice, wife and baby, your Uncle Robert making his bed on the floor with the carriage cushions and a buffalo robe which had been purchased at Shawneetown. He evidently felt relieved that he was not under the necessity of getting into the infected beds. Although I did not believe there was any danger, I took the precaution to spread some pocket-handkerchiefs over the pillows, and by only removing my outside garments and putting on gloves, a thing I could not induce your father to do, felt pretty secure as to infection, but not quite comfortable as respected the mood of mine host. Being very tired I thought I would lie down, but not allow myself to sleep. Our trunks were deposited in the same room where we were, and I imagined that there had been a suspicious eyeing throughout the evening, and that the inside as well as the out might prove attractive; as we were so evidently in close quarters with a mad man, was not altogether at ease about our personal safety. I was very tired, and Morpheus finally overcame all my resolutions and made me forgetful of danger.

I do not know how long I had slept, when aroused by the crying of baby and the coarse swearing of the father. He scolded his wife for letting it cry, and then cursed the "little imp; imp of the devil." The wife said the child needed caring for, and would not go to sleep without it; that it must be taken to the fire and made dry and comfortable, but he swore he would gag the squalling brat. After a while he sprang out of bed and pulling the child from under the bed clothes, declared he would roast it. There was in the fire-place a large fire, made of oak logs, which were all aglow and gave light to the whole room. He took the baby under one arm, and with two or three bounds was at the fire-place. He commenced raking open the coals, still holding baby under his arm, swearing he would make a back-log; "yes, I'll brile ye." I kept both eyes open and trembled for the fate of the baby, when, to my surprise, he seated himself, carefully warmed the dry linen that was hanging by the fire, and in the most handy manner performed all that a good nurse or mother could have done. And now that baby was dry and there was no good reason for crying, and swearing did not soothe, he pressed "the brat, imp of the devil," to his breast, and commenced singing a good Methodist hymn in a soft, subdued voice, and had it been my first impression I should have supposed him a most devout Christian. A more sudden change from the profane to the devotional could not be imagined.

This scene occurred forty-eight years ago, and now it is as fresh to my mind as at that time, but perfectly to describe it would be impossible. The most provoking part of the last performance was that I had to enjoy it alone; no one to share with me the ludicrous climax of the closing hymn, your father and Uncle Robert being asleep. As soon as it was light we were up and ready for a leave-taking. At the five-mile house on the other side of the swamp we found a plain, decent family, who gave us a breakfast of "common doings," corn bread and bacon, without any attempt at "wheat bread and chicken fixings," and from them we heard more of Brice Hanna. The man told us that Brice had a good farm and in his way kept his family comfortable, took pride in having the best wagon and horses in the county. He had always been proud of his wives, the one we saw being his third, but his greatest pride was in his peculiar capacity for swearing. He once took an oath that he would not swear again for two years, from the

fact that he had found a man down in "Shawnee" who could out-swear him, and he said he
felt mean ever after. He was true to his vow,
but when the two years had expired commenced with renewed vigor. The gossip of
the settlement was that his first wife died of a
broken heart, that he had poisoned the second,
and that the poor young creature whom we
saw had jumped into the well to drown herself,
but the water not being deep, was pulled out
with nothing but bruises for her effort. The
man did not believe the story of his having
poisoned his second wife, but thought what was
reported of the last might be true.

We had left Shawneetown on Saturday with
the feeling that it was no place to spend the
Sabbath, and finding ourselves at a worse place
at night, we did not think it amiss to move on
Sunday morning. At the place where we
breakfasted they told us there was no place of
preaching near, but on the other side of the
prairie they had preaching every Sunday in a
schoolhouse, so there being no place here to
stay longer than to breakfast and to rest our
horses, we set our faces northward again, and
soon after starting came to a large prairie; I
think it was called "Hind's prairie." This
was my first introduction to a real prairie, and
I must say I was sorely disappointed. Your
father had talked so much about their beauty
that I expected to feel a kind of enchantment.
He said, "you never saw anything like this be-

fore." I said "no;" but did not say I never saw anything more dismal; and to those who have seen western prairies after the autumnal fires have passed over, leaving them in all their blackness, with an occasional strip of coarse grass or a scrubby bush, it will be needless to describe, and I think hard to gather beauties from it.

We did not reach a stopping place until dark. Found a cabin with one room, the two heads alone being at home. The "younguns," as the mother said, had gone to preaching at the schoolhouse, two miles off. We felt no inclination to follow and join in the services, although they said that the "greatest preacher in the sarkit was to be thar." The people all thought a "power of him," and he was "doing a heap of good." They gave us a clean, coarse supper; had neither coffee nor "store tea," but what they call "mountain tea," made from some herb that grew in that region. It had a pleasant taste, and with appetites sharpened by hunger and thirst we made a very refreshing meal, and were soon snugly occupying the one-legged bedstead that stood in the corner of the cabin. If I had endurance to write all I would like, I would tell of some of the freaks of one-legged bedsteads, and also give a description of them.

I do not recollect where we stopped Monday night, but remember a place where we called about noon on Tuesday, and the mis-

take I made. As we went into the yard a little
boy with no other garment on than a shirt was
mounted on a large white horse, while two
larger boys, in shirts and pants, were driving
the horse around the house. I thought they
were imposing on their little brother and
stopped to ask them not to tease him in that
way, and to get his clothes and let him dress
himself. Your father looked amused, and said
I had come too late in the season to see the
prairie boys "turned into their shirts," a western custom of which I will speak hereafter.
Your father called for a pitcher of milk, but
the pitcher with the one tumbler furnished was
sufficient for me; I can see them now as they
then looked in their filth.

Thursday, November 26, we arrived at a
very comfortable looking two-story log house,
just before sunset. The outward appearance
of the establishment indicated that they — as
the westerners say — "were in a better fix" than
most of their neighbors, so we anticipated a
good supper, but I saw the lady — as she called
herself — go through the whole process of preparing the meal, which satisfied all my cravings
for supper, though my appetite had been well
sharpened by a day's ride. I could relate a
queer experience, but am getting along slowly
in my week's travel from "Shawnee." Your
father not knowing the reason why I could not
eat supper, being out with the host during the
preparations, asked for an early breakfast, as

we might not find as good a place on the way. Oh, dear, what could I do? In vain I urged him to start before breakfast, but he could see no reason for so doing, and I in presence of host and hostess could not explain.

Tired and supperless I went to bed, and "nature's sweet restorer" soon came to my relief. I awoke early, and perceiving through the chintz curtains that hung around our bed, that there was light in the room, hastened to awake your father, and urged him to get off without waiting for breakfast. He peered through the loop-holes, and with much satisfaction told me it was the fire-light I saw, and they were preparing our breakfast. Oh, oh, oh! what could I do? I told him it would be impossible for me to eat a mouthful in that house, and that what I had seen the night before was already more than I could stand; but before we were ready to start breakfast was smoking on the table, and I had no alternative but to sit down. Fortunately the lady thought I might be sick, and rummaging somewhere brought me a cracker, which, with some honey-comb that was on the table, made an apology for a breakfast. Hunger had so far gained the ascendancy that I would not look to see the place where the cracker had been deposited.

We were soon ready to take up our line of travel, and to say farewell to our hosts. Mine host, by the way, was no mean personage; talked politics, did not swear; said he had been thinking of running for the legislature; seemed to be in good humor with every one — particularly himself. Mine hostess had children from boys of sixteen or eighteen to the wee baby sitting on the floor, with a darkey of the masculine gender for a nurse; said nurse was about as large as a good-sized dog, and could act dog or monkey, as best suited baby's whims; so having a darkey she was a mistress, consequently a lady. When we were again on our way I had the time to review the incidents of the past week. Shawneetown, the encounter with the stump at our watering place, Brice Hanna, the poverty, ignorance, and filthiness of the people I had met, the black dismal prairie I had crossed, suffering from pinching hunger, and, with feelings better imagined than described, was feeling that the farther I went the worse things I might have to encounter. When your father said ''the breakfast seemed pretty good,'' I asked him if he thought it had time to digest? If so, I would tell him of a few things that went to make his meal.

After leaving Shawneetown we had been traveling in a northwesterly direction, making a circuitous route in order to head the water courses, there being no bridges in those days. On Wednesday, about noon, we came to the Kaskaskia River, where there was a rope ferry. I had never seen anything like it before — believe it is called cordelling.

February 1, 1871.

Have not been able, on account of my rheumatic infirmity, to write for several weeks, and I cannot make up my mind to read over what I have written of late, but imagine that although true to the letter it is fidgety, partaking of my uncomfortable temperament at the time I wrote, for I was looking back to the dark events of nearly fifty years' standing under the shadow that dyspeptic eyes can cast over even things cheering. I will endeavor to forget the trivial perplexities that were so vividly occupying my mind at that time. I have been enabled through the most of my sickness to keep a bright future, and think I still do, but so many weaknesses, dyspeptic troubles, my irritating cough and bronchial difficulties, and of late rheumatic twinges, all conspire to make me momentarily desponding and cause me to bury myself under a heavy cloud. I rejoice that the cloud soon passes away, and that I am left to meditate on the loving kindness that has always surrounded me. Cast down, but through the loving kindness of my gentle Shepherd, I feel that I am not forgotten or uncared for.

From the Kaskaskia River we proceeded to the town of Carlyle, the county seat of Clinton County, where we found several frame houses, the first I had seen after leaving Shawneetown. We drove up to a comfortable looking frame tavern, and were ushered into their dining room, where was a nice fire of hickory wood, with a clean brick hearth, which had evidently been washed that day; brass andirons, too, clean and bright. I had only time to divest myself of my outer wrapping when dinner was brought in. The nice roast chickens with all their accompaniments were prepared in Yankee style, and set on a nicely washed and ironed table cloth, to say nothing of the peach pie, and sundry other things. Did I not luxuriate? I do not think I am particularly given to gormandizing, but after such loathing of food for a week and dire starvation, that dinner and the tidiness and comfort that reigned in that dwelling is so indelibly impressed on my mind as never to be forgotten.

After dinner we rode twenty miles to Greenville, the county seat of Bond County. I went with a lighter heart after being fed, and feeling, too, that I was not entirely beyond the bounds of civilization. At Greenville, where we arrived a little after dark, we went to the Blanchards', the Stoughton, Massachusetts, family of whom I have before spoken. Mr. Blanchard was walking the floor with his little daughter to keep her from crying, and thereby disturb her mother, who was in the room above, and had an infant a few days old. After supper we received calls from Benjamin Mills and Dr. Newhall, who had heard of our arrival, and came over from their respective offices; also from Mr.

and Mrs. Birge, who lived in a small brick building opposite. Mr. Birge had a store, and was postmaster of Bond County. They lived in the only brick house in the county. Mrs. Birge was a sister of Mrs. Blanchard. Their visit was ostensibly a congratulatory one, and all seemed much pleased to see your father; but I was also much amused to perceive the curiosity at work in investigating what kind of a wife Tillson had brought out. Your Uncle Robert, too, was thoroughly scanned.

In the morning I was invited up to see Mrs. Blanchard, who was sitting up in bed with her hair in long ringlets, and looking as if she never could be nervous. We then started for our home, being only twenty miles from our destination. We crossed one of the forks of Shoal Creek, which was then fordable, and a long prairie, then entered the timber land which bordered another fork of the creek. Winding through the woods without any road, we at last came out on a public road, just opened between Vandalia and Springfield, and soon came in sight of our future home, our log house, enclosed, as you will see in my rough drawing, by a fence. It was situated on the top of a high bluff from which there was a steep descent on the south, reaching to what was termed the bottom, and where your father afterwards made what he called his "bottom farm." He built a cabin thereon, and rented it to Billy Buzan.

Arrived at the house, we were met by a horseman who said he had been on the lookout for us for several days. I was then formally introduced to Mr. Shurtleff. I had heard your father speak of him. He addressed me as an old acquaintance and said he knew my father well, which knowledge I afterwards found to be that my father, being colonel of a militia regiment, once a year at ''muster'' the colonel inspected the several companies belonging to the regiment, and Shurtleff, being a private in a Carver company, saw my father every time the inspection took place; hence his acquaintance with me. Your father, previous to leaving Massachusetts, had written Mr. Rountree that he should take back a wife and a brother, and wanted him to remain in the house and board us through the winter. Not hearing from him, had supposed it was all arranged as he wished; he had also written to have a kitchen built in the rear of the house for Mr. Rountree's benefit, while we were to occupy the house.

Judge of my surprise when on entering to find the house without any vestige of furniture, excepting the front bedroom, where little Major Black was in full possession. In ''the office'' was the old desk and book-case which John now has in Quincy, two writing desks, a sheet-iron stove, and four split-bottomed chairs. The room had one window and a puncheon floor. Mr. Black said Mr. Rountree had received your father's letter, but had finished his cabin and moved into it, leaving him with a few quarts of corn-meal in a bag, and a handful of salt done up in a newspaper. There had been quite an amount of money paid into the office, brought up from St. Louis in specie to pay the non-resident taxes, and as Mr. Black had not deemed it safe to leave the premises even long enough to get a meal, he had lived on roasted potatoes, seasoned with the salt that had been left him, and slaked his thirst from the deep well in front of the house. He had a mattress and a couple of blankets belonging to your father, and these with a buffalo robe served for pillow, sheets, and covering.

Mr. Rountree had rented the ground under the peach trees and made a "truck patch;" had divided the products, depositing your father's share of potatoes, turnips, and cabbage under the floor, which was fortunate for Mr. Black in his extremity. Mr. Black said that Colonel Seward had been down, and left word for us to go to his house and remain until ours could be made ready for occupancy; as had also Mr. Townsend, the Rev. Jesse. I sat in the office with Mr. Black while your father went to Jesse Buzan's and engaged board for Black and your Uncle Robert, arranging so that one could stay in the office while the other went to his meals. While this was going on, Mr. Shurtleff had cleared our carriage of everything contained therein and brought them into the house, carefully examining every trunk and parcel; and although he lived the nearest of anyone to our dwelling, never once hinted our taking a meal with him, though he well knew we had not taken food after leaving Greenville in the morning. So when your father was ready to start for Colonel Seward's, the trunks had to be taken back to the carriage.

We arrived at the Seward's, three miles from our place, about sunset. Mrs. Seward, a dear, good woman, and Harriet, now Mrs. Wm. H. Brown of Chicago, were the only members of the family at home. Before our evening meal was ready the Colonel with his boy, John, arrived from Vandalia. The legislature having removed from Kaskaskia, were to hold their first session at Vandalia that winter,[14] and Israel Seward Jr., with his wife and niece, Sally Slayback, had taken a house there to board members of the legislature, leaving their two older children, William and George, with their grandfather. The old Colonel was all smiles and gave me a most cordial welcome,

[14] Vandalia, created capital of Illinois by the fiat of the first state legislature, at the time lay eighty miles in the wilderness. Extravagant expectations were at first entertained concerning the growth of the town thus created. These were disappointed, and several years before the close of the twenty-year period for which the capital had been fixed at Vandalia, rival towns were seeking to secure the coveted prize. It finally went to Springfield, due to the scheming of a group of legislators from Sangamon County, in which Abraham Lincoln bore a prominent part.

75

as had also Mrs. and Miss Seward; and it was a cordial to my feelings, particularly after my introduction and experience with my nearest neighbor. I wish I could describe him as I first saw him in front of the house. Imagine a very tall, lank man, with his legs encased in a pair of linsey pantaloons, rough and dirty; over these, leggings that came above the knees, made from an old bed-blanket and tied up with some buckskin strings; then an old drab overcoat and a shabby hat; a saddle girth tied around his waist, and a coarse, woolen scarf around his neck, and all dirty. So many such personages presented themselves, welcoming your father back, that I should not particularly remember his appearance had not my first impressions been strengthened by further acquaintance.

It was the twenty-eighth of November when we arrived at Colonel Seward's, and I had a more homelike feeling than for many weeks. We had a clean, comfortable meal, Mother Seward and Harriet each performing their part in the domestic duties, while the Colonel talked politics and discussed the affairs of the state. Their house was about the size of ours, but had not been divided by any partitions. On the opposite side from the fireplace were two beds, standing foot to foot; there was a square frame over each, from which were suspended curtains that went around the front and foot of each bed. The curtains were so arranged as to leave about a foot of space between the bed and curtain, to which we could pin our dresses, and by inexpansiveness could stand within the curtain and feel that we had all the privacy of a dressing room. One of the beds was for the Colonel and his wife and we had the other, while Harriet slept in a small bed, which, during the day, was rolled under the Colonel's.

After breakfast Friday morning your father went down to the office, and said he should not return until Saturday night. I had a pleasant, quiet day with Mrs. Seward and Harriet. Towards night it began to snow and blow, and as I stood by the window — the house had but one — watching the storm, a loud rapping announced the arrival of more company. Miss Harriet opened the door and ushered in two respectable-looking gentlemen. One she introduced as Mr. Conover; although I well remember the looks of the other, I cannot recall his name; but as if it had occurred yesterday I remember how he divested himself of his leggings and buffalo overshoes, and with what a satisfied look he gazed at the fire and took a survey of the room. They were members of the legislature from Sangamon, on their way to Vandalia. Before we had finished our evening meal Mrs. Butler Seward came to call on me. She lived about a quarter of a mile from the Colonel's, in the same grove. As they had other company at the Colonel's she invited Harriet and myself to return with her and pass the night, so we went, Harriet rising while it was yet dark to go home and assist her mother, while I remained to breakfast.

Saturday night your father came up, bringing the carriage, and said he would take us all to "preaching" the next day.

Sunday morning, December 2, was cold and pinching; winter had commenced in earnest. We rode about two miles to a log cabin which, during week days, was the schoolhouse of the village or settlement schoolmaster, and Sundays was open to the "circuit rider,"—Methodist preacher,—who came around "onst" a month, and to the "Cumberlands,"—Cumberland Presbyterians,—who occasionally preached there; also to the "Hard-shells," and to the "Seventh-day" Baptists—all were tolerated. When we arrived the service had just commenced; a movement was made to give Harriet and myself a seat by the fire, while your father posted himself on one of the schoolhouse benches that stood against the wall. The preacher, big and burly, was about starting the hymn, which was done by reading the first two lines of the verse, and then with an indescribable nasal twang, singing to the tune of "Old Grimes," the lines that had been repeated. This was a favorite among them:

"When I can read my titul clare,
Tue mansheons in the skei,
I'll bid farewell to everie fear,
And wipe my weeping ye, yi, yi,
and wipe" &c.

Around the fire sat the mothers with babies, while the "young'uns" huddled down on the floor beside them. In the circle where we were put there seemed to be a mixture of all ages, though of but one sex; the lords of creation with their big boys occupying the back seats. After the sermon—if so it may be called—the preacher sang another "hyme," the congregation chiming in. It was then announced that after a few minutes' recess another brother would speak; then commenced the performance. The "young'uns" rushed to the fire with sticks or pieces of clapboard and rolled out the eggs they had brought for a lunch and had deposited in the ashes to roast while the first preacher was speaking. Each youngster worked manfully to secure his own rights, and showed dispatch of business in getting them peeled and disposed of before the preaching was resumed. The good mammas who had babies, and who did not wait for recess, but had been giving them their lunch during the service, now lit their pipes and looked so happy and satisfied as the clouds of smoke curled out from under their sunbonnets, meanwhile the sterner sex paying suit to the water bucket which stood in the back corner of the room; that performance was rather slow, there being but one gourd shell for the whole congregation, so each man would walk up to the bucket and while another was drinking would relieve his mouth of a heavy quid, holding it in one hand, would take the gourd of water, rinse his mouth, spitting the washing on the floor, then take his drink, and while passing the gourd to the next would throw his "bacca" in his mouth and be ready for a chat.

The preaching had commenced at ten A. M., and it was not until between four and five o'clock that we were released from the rant. I had never before heard but one Methodist preach, and that was Father Taylor, in the early part of his ministry. He in New England was in those days considered a "ranter," but if his preaching was rant, surely our western Methodism was ranting outranted.

The order of preaching was for the first speaker to be somewhat logical, and to show forth to the listening audience his great learning and wisdom; for the last speaker was left the sensational. He would "get happy," clap his hands, froth at the mouth; the congregation responding, some groaning, some crying loudly, "Amen," some calling "glory, glory, glory to God!" When I look back on these meetings now, I can recollect but one impression that was left on my mind; that of intense disgust. If these preachers had come among the people meekly, and with an earnest desire to do good to the souls of men — however weak and ignorant they might have been — I could have respected their effort, and felt a sympathy in their performances, but their whole manner evinced so much arrogance and

self-display and such unblushing impudence as
to repel me.

As we came out from preaching I was introduced to Mr. Jesse Buzan, who had married
'Squire Davy's daughter, Peggy. Jesse invited us to his house to dinner, which invitation
we accepted. The furniture in his cabin consisted of one bed, a spinning-wheel, six chairs
and a table; some rude shelves on the wall held
the dishes, while the Dutch oven and the frying-
pan found a place on the floor under the shelves.
Jesse had taken a bee-line through the woods,
and met us at the door when we arrived, with
his baby in his arms, and as we went in he
smilingly looked at his wife and said, ''Paygie,
this heur is Mrs. Tillson.'' Peggy, who stood
at the table with her hands in the dough, gave
a grunt and said, ''how gey,'' then looking at
Harriet gave another grunt and again said,
''how gey.'' Jesse then looked at Peggy and
said inquiringly, ''I reckon they can put their
fixin's on the bed.'' Peggy said, ''I allow,'' so
we deposited our bonnets and cloaks on the
''blue kiver'' that kivered the bed, and then
took our seats by the fire. Peggy seemed in-
tent on her cooking and had nothing to say.
Jesse told your father about his ''craps,'' and
evidently felt very rich; said he was ''getting
on right smart;'' it had been a good mast
year — an abundance of nuts — and his hogs
had come out of the woods fat enough to kill.
He thought by another winter he should be

able to sit by the fire most of the time. Poor child of nature, thought I; and your wants, how few. I looked around the cabin to see what attraction there could be for Jesse the coming year. Peggy was disagreeably ugly, but Jesse said she was good for work and that was what he wanted, "for, if she was dressed up, she couldn't look pretty, no how."

I looked to see if there were any books —an old almanac, begrimmed and greasy, hanging against the wall, was all the literature offered. But Jesse and Peggy "didn't want books;" did not think it was of "any use to be allus reading;" "didn't think folks was any better off for reading, an' books cost a heap and took a power of time;" "twant so bad for men to read, for there was a heap of time when they couldn't work out, and could jest set by the fire; and if a man had books and keered to read he mought; but women had no business to hurtle away their time, case they could allus find something to du, and there had been a heap of trouble in old Kaintuck with some rich men's gals that had learned to write. They was sent to school, and were high larnt, and cud write letters almost as well as a man, and would write to the young fellows, and, bless your soul, get a match fixed up before their father or mother knowed a hait about it." Such were Jesse's honest sentiments, and such was the standard of at least nine-tenths of the inhabitants that were our neighbors.

Jesse's conversation was interrupted by the entrance of a handsome young man, dressed in a suit of blue broadcloth: it had been, probably, two years before a very genteel suit; but time and constant service had left their marks, and it required no effort of imagination to decide that he was white at the elbows. I discovered he came by invitation to meet and dine with us. Jesse went through the ceremony of introduction, then turning to Mr. Porter, said: "See here, Porter, I'll get you to nurse while I run down to the bottom of the field to see if the fence is all right;" and suiting the action to the word, dropped Matilda into Mr. Porter's lap. Poor Porter! he blushed, looked at us, looked at Matilda as if he wished her among the hickory logs in the big fire-place; but as nothing could be said or done, he seemed to be meekly growing into submission to his fate, when Miss Harriet had the benevolence to go and relieve him of his charge, rallying him at the same time for his awkwardness.

Jesse went and returned, Peggy put her last dish on the table, and dinner was announced. The table was high, coming up to our chins; the chairs low, and we were obliged to sit with our arms akimbo, in order to manage our knives and forks. The table was covered with a coarse cloth, five plates were set around, the sixth bearing the burden of Peggy's heavy biscuits; a teacup and iron spoon beside each plate, the sixth cup holding some salt, and the sixth saucer was for the butter. A platter with some fried ham and another with some honeycomb completed the meal. Soon the invited guests were all seated when Jesse, handing Matilda to Peggy, took the head of the table; and Peggy, with the baby on her hip, took the cups from the table and with a tin cup filled them with coffee from the Dutch oven in which it had been made. This hot beverage, sweetened with maple sugar, was not to be slighted after our long fast. Jesse seemed happy in presiding; praised the bacon; said "it was from a mighty fine shoat; that he hated mightily to kill it, but we can't live without bacon nohow, though I don't mind if I can have plenty of mush and milk. Peggy she says she despises to make mush, it is such a spite to clean the mushpot. When I go to the crock for milk, Peggy tells me to blow back the cream. Wall, ye see, I do it, and then dip my milk out of the side that has the cream." Then he chuckled at his own wit. Peggy meantime took a chair before the fire and gave baby its dinner. When our cups were to be replenished Jesse gave Peggy the watchword, who would take our cups to the fire and bring them back filled, baby nothing moved by the act.

Well, I have told you all the particulars of my first dining out, and will not go into details of another, as that was the style, and the best the "white folks" could do. As I had to accept many invitations of the kind, and with the same etiquette, lest the neighbors might think us proud, you may imagine the pleasure I took in visiting. The Townsends and Sewards, New Yorkers, were the only families who had any better notions of what belonged to refinement and comfort within twenty miles; at Greenville were the Blanchards and Birges.

We remained at Colonel Seward's about two weeks. During the time your father had initiated your Uncle Robert into the office, taken Mr. Black to Vandalia and recommended him to a clerkship in the Auditor's office, where he remained several years. Poor Black was in a sad plight to present himself before the great officials at the capital. He had but his last New York suit, which was sadly tattered. I found a coat which your father had cast aside because it was too small, and by brushing it up and making a few repairs it was quite a passable garment. The pantaloons did not suit as well; his little limbs seemed lost in their broad dimensions.

"A world too wide were they for his shrunk shank."

Mr. Black had the most exquisite taste and his clothing had been of the nicest kind, and he had been very fastidious about their fit. But all was gone, and the coarse brogans had to take the place of the dainty, well-polished boot. I should like to tell you of his first experience while trying to become an Illinois

85

farmer. It is a tragic story, but if I stop to tell it I shall not reach St. Louis. If strength is spared me I will write it out with other things that occurred.

I will not stop to relate any of the oddities of old Colonel Seward. He was always pleasant to me, and after we were in the carriage starting for St. Louis he came to say he was sorry we could not have stayed longer and very confidentially told us that next week Mr. Brown and Harriet were going to be married. I had suspected that something was brewing, but Mrs. Seward and Harriet had hinted nothing, and so did not feel particularly flattered by the Colonel's invitation; I think, however, they would have been glad to have had us, but with one room, and company expected from St. Louis, what could they do? and I felt glad to relieve them by vacating a small corner of the cabin. Perhaps I will write more of the wedding, whereon I could hang another story. We took our trunks and all the paraphernalia of our wanderings down to our own house, where we opened a trunk that had been the depository for our soiled clothing, having had but one washing done since leaving home — nearly three months before. I asked your father if he had a large trunk with a good lock, where I could leave things to remain undisturbed during our absence; he had. So I filled a bag of things to be washed whenever the time arrived, and gave it to your father to take up the ladder to the trunk, asking again about the lock. When I turned around I saw, standing bolt upright, my tall friend, watching the bag and looking determined to know its contents — another tale to be told.

We arrived at Rev. Jesse Townsend's about sunset, nine miles on our way to St. Louis. The family were absent, excepting Mrs. Townsend with her son Edwin and wife. Mr. Townsend had gone to Edwardsville to establish a school; Eleazer and wife to spend the winter at Vandalia. The house was cheery and comfortable. A large family room with two bedrooms opening out of it, a hall with another small bedroom at the side, a kitchen separate from the house, with an awning, where in the summer they spread their table and took their meals; rooms all carpeted with bag carpeting, old tables and chairs brought from Palmyra, New York, and books in abundance. It was truly heart-cheering, and made me feel that there might yet be some comfort in living in Illinois. Mrs. Townsend the elder was a woman of intelligence, but had been sick, and was not sanguine about Illinois; Mrs. Townsend the younger was a sweet-tempered, loving woman, who probably had, from many causes, more reasons for repining than the mother; she was very cordial, and I made up my mind at once to like her, and never had cause to change my feelings toward her. She was a Miss Durfee, from Palmyra, New York.

A Woman's Story

We went the next day to Edwardsville, thirty-five miles; stopped at Major Hopkins', who kept hotel. The Major was a son of General Hopkins of northern New York, who had been an influential man but had lost his property, and had died, leaving a widow and two children, Miss Polly and the Major. They had removed to Illinois with small means for a beginning, but with all the feelings of dignity that their former position had given them. Madam was a lady of the old school, and a real lady; intelligent, dignified, and with most decidedly religious principles, which she never put in compromise. Miss Polly was smart and energetic, but with such a high seasoning of sarcasm that it was said she was the terror of all gentlemen, and maintained her own independent single blessedness for more than forty years. Her brother, the Major, was a pleasant little gentleman, with all the polish and civility of a Frenchman. He had married a Cincinnati girl, lovely-tempered and a good housekeeper, whose common sense and watchfulness was much needed in such a family. At the table we met the Rev. Mr. Townsend, at whose house we had been entertained the previous night, and Hooper Warren and wife. Mr. Warren was editor of the Edwardsville *Spectator*, and had just married a Miss Adamson of Louisville; also a son of Captain Breath, of the Marine settlement, who afterwards became a missionary and died in Syria; I think he was cousin to the Leggetts'.

From Edwardsville we started for St. Louis, only twenty miles, but owing to the bad traveling did not reach the Mississippi River until just before sunset. The ice was running in the river so that the ferryboat had not been used for several days, and passengers were taken over in a skiff. Not knowing the danger to which we would be exposed, we went into the skiff, your father, myself, and a gentleman who had come with us from Edwardsville, and we were pushed off into the mighty river. Two men acted as rowers, while two others stood with long poles to turn aside the huge piles of ice which would at times rush upon the boat, and it seemed as if nothing could save us, and while one was being shoved away another would be bearing down and stop all movement. The boatmen—if I had not previously heard from Brice Hanna, the finishing of all profanity—I should have thought the most wicked and hardened men I had ever met, swearing at each other and swearing at the great banks of ice, challenging each as they came in contact with our boat to keep out of the way or they would send them to a place "whar" ice did not grow.

When we arrived at St. Louis people would hardly believe that we had crossed the river that day, as it was at the risk of life to make the attempt, and I began to more fully realize the danger through which we had passed; and now, when I look back and think of the hair-breadth escapes I was carried through in my early journeyings, it leads me to inquire for what purpose and end was I spared? I have been but an unprofitable servant in the vineyard of Him whom I have proposed to serve.

We spent about two weeks in St. Louis, putting up at Mrs. Paddock's, who kept a boarding house. She was from Middleborough, Massachusetts. Her husband was on a farm in Illinois and a part of the family were with him, while Madame Paddock presided over the St. Louis establishment. They had eight daughters and one son, the youngest child, then a lad in a store in St. Louis, afterwards a merchant at Springfield, Illinois, where Mrs. Enos, one of the daughters, lived. Mr. Enos[15] was appointed receiver of public moneys under John Quincy

[15] Pascal P. Enos was a citizen of Connecticut who came west to Cincinnati in 1815 and the following year continued his migration to St. Charles, Missouri. From 1817 to 1821 he lived in St. Louis, removing thence to Madison County, Illinois, six miles north of Edwardsville. Mr. Enos was appointed by President Monroe receiver of the land office for the Sangamon district. In 1823 he joined with Elijah Iles, John Taylor, and Thomas Cox in entering land and laying out a townsite to which the name "Calhoun" was given. For some reason this name was soon displaced by that of "Springfield." Mr. Enos died at Springfield, which he had thus helped to found, in 1832. His wife was living at Springfield as late as 1874, being then in her eighty-fifth year.

Adams, to whom he was said to bear a strong personal likeness. His daughter, Miss Enos, married Mr. Hatch of Springfield. William Porter, who nursed Peggy's baby, was employed by Mr. Enos as a clerk in his office, a situation more adapted to his style than holding babies.

At St. Louis everything seemed strange, and to me new. The gentlemen were from every part of the Union, and those with whom I met were indeed gentlemen, and there was occasionally to be found a lady, mostly from among the eastern emigration. The French Catholic ladies, with their heaps of expensive finery and a darkey to attend them whenever they went into the street, were to me a subject of study, and the more I studied the more prejudiced I became. At the table I met the three brothers Kerr; they were all single, but afterwards married, and we always kept up an acquaintance with them, particularly Mr. and Mrs. Augustus Kerr. Mrs. Kerr was a very lovely lady—a Philadelphian. They visited us when you were not quite a year old and Mr. Kerr, who was foolishly fond of children and had none of his own, said he had seen nothing in Boston he cared to appropriate unless it was the baby girl of mine. Mr. Elliot was another with whom I became acquainted. He kept a large store for St. Louis at that time, and I purchased my crockery of him. After we had made our purchases he invited us into the back room, a kind of sitting room. There was a table in the middle of the room, with wine, oranges, nuts, coffee, and all the nice things the market afforded. It was a preparation for us. He had known your father, and seemed also to take a "mighty liking" to his wife; hence the parade.

One day I wanted something from the store and went to Mr. Clemens, on the same street with my boarding house, made my purchase, took my small parcel, and was turning to go out, when Mr. Clemens inquired if I was unattended. Finding I was, he took his hat, whirled himself over the counter, and escorted me to Mrs. Paddock's door. I thought it a stretch of southern politeness, but later I knew more of the habits of the St. Louisians, and that only a few years before the red men had been occupants of the country around, and that their visits were still frequent and unceremonious, not bringing the southern gallantry to ladies to bear on their advances. Pretty squaw was their most gracious salutation, and that only when they discovered some trinket about a lady's dress that they wished to appropriate, and which was often obtained by dint of flattery. Mr. Clemens was at that time a suitor of Miss Julia Paddock's, who was a great beauty and the flower of the family. She did not accept the heart and hand of Mr. Clemens, but afterwards married Mr. B., of Springfield. Mr. Clemens married into the rich Mullanphy family, where with his broad acres, his negroes, and his French Catholic wife, he became absorbed in his own circle, and has not mixed with the American population since.

Mr. John Warburton was also a boarder in the house, and being a Connecticut Yankee we became acquainted and continued a friendly intercourse through his life. He died a few years ago at Hartford, his native place, having amassed quite a fortune and sustained a high character as a business man and as a decided Christian gentleman.

The first Sabbath after we arrived a handsome young gentleman called and invited us to attend church. We accepted the invitation and went with him to a small building on Fourth Street, considered at that time a little out in the country. The room was used for a Presbyterian church on the Sabbath, and was the only one in St. Louis. The preacher was Rev. Salmon Giddings, a graduate of Williams College, where he had also been a tutor.[16] He

[16] The Rev. Salmon Giddings, a Connecticut man, was the founder of Presbyterianism in St. Louis. Appointed a missionary, he rode horseback 1,200 miles in the winter of 1815-16, arriving at St. Louis in April, 1816. Before his death in 1828 he had organized many Presbyterian churches in the city (the first in November, 1817) and gained a remarkable hold on its population. His funeral was attended by 2,000 people, half the population of the city. When the First Presbyterian church was dedicated in 1855, a funeral hymn was sung immediately after the sermon, and during the singing Rev. Mr. Giddings' body was carried in and deposited in a vault beneath the pulpit.

was then a bachelor, but afterwards the husband of Miss Almira Collins and the father of Frederic Giddings of Quincy. Mr. Giddings used the room on the Sabbath, and through the week our escort—who was no other than Henry H. Snow, afterwards of Quincy—presided over a school of young ladies. These young misses were from the aristocratic families of St. Louis and Mr. Snow—a handsome young man and a fine singer—was quite a favorite among them. He led the singing at the church. Mrs. Paddock, who in her young days had been a singer, and was still fond of music, invited Mr. Snow several times to her house to meet your father, and one evening had quite a company, apologizing to the southern guests for getting up, instead of a dance, a psalm-singing, explaining that psalm-singing was a Yankee amusement.

The Paddocks were smart, excellent housekeepers; knew how to make their household arrangements comfortable and elegant; could converse sensibly, appeared well at a dance, were kind to friends, but horribly severe upon what they termed Yankee bigotry in matters of religion. They called themselves Universalists, and I am sorry to say did not do much to honor their Puritan training. The next Sabbath we went to a little Methodist chapel, the only Protestant place of worship in St. Louis with the exception of Judge Snow's school-room. The pulpit was supplied by an

English gentleman named Keyte, who preached Methodism on Sunday and sold goods through the week. He was of the firm of Tiffany & Keyte. Mr. Tiffany was from Attleboro, Massachusetts; he afterwards moved to Baltimore, and is the father of the Rev. Mr. Tiffany of Chicago. Tiffany and Keyte sustained a good reputation both as business men and Christians.

When we left St. Louis we took with us a servant girl—a "Kaintuck"—and arrived at our place of abode on the afternoon of January 3. I am tired now, and must take a rest, and then will try to look into our house as it presented itself on that memorable afternoon of January 3, 1823.

After Mr. Black had left the office, and during our absence, William Loomis, a carpenter, had been employed to build a flight of stairs in one corner of the room, in place of the ladder, and to finish the kitchen. He was to board at Jesse Buzan's and to sleep at the house with Robert. The management worked well for a while, but for some reason they decided to give up boarding and keep "bachelor's hall." They had managed to get a Dutch oven and a frying pan, the former for baking their corn bread and the frying pan for cooking their meat; they had roasted their potatoes in the ashes. They had a cow, which furnished them with milk and butter. They managed the dairy by taking one of the large, square bottles that had been left by Simpson,

and filling it with milk, set it aside for drinking.
Then they took another bottle to hold what
was called the strippings—the richest part,
containing the cream. First I should have
said having no milk-pail, they had milked from
the cow into the bottle. Their process of
turning the "strippings" to butter, was to sit
and shake the bottle, Loomis shaking until he
was tired and then passing it over to Robert,
who took his turn. When the butter "kum,"
as Loomis termed it, they salted it with some
of the Rountree salt, and using the buttermilk
as a beverage, they sat down to what Loomis
called a most onexcellent meal.

However "onexcellent" their meals might
have been, surely elegance did not reign in the
cabin. In the center of the room stood the
work-bench, and the floor was covered with
shavings about a foot deep. Loomis, good
soul! was always kind and obliging, but his
infirmity it was to have an imaginary story to
tell when the truth would have been quite as
convenient. He began by saying that they
had expected us home every night for the last
week and had swept the floor and put everything in good order for our reception, produc-
ing a broom that they had manufactured. But
that day they had been out to get more tallow
for making candles. Your father remarked
that he had made a good many shavings in one
day, besides so much candle and butter making.
Loomis looked confused and went on to clean

the room. Loomis and Robert took down the work-bench and removed it to the kitchen, while I, in my green traveling-dress and hood, with broom in hand made war upon the swamp of shavings that still carpeted the puncheon floor. Your father in the meantime had gone over to Shurtleff's, and bought a shoulder of pork. He brought it home just as the teams from St. Louis arrived with—in western phrase—our plunder.

The room was cleaned, and we were in a fair way to get up another "onexcellent" supper, when Loomis told us they had used the last candle the night before, but there was some deer tallow and some wicking he had got from old Davy's, and some molds he had brought with himself. So cooking operations were suspended. I arranged the wick on the moulds, while Joicy, the girl we had brought with us, was melting the deer tallow in the frying pan at the fire-place. The moulds were soon filled and set by the door to cool, and Joicy washed the frying pan and commenced the cooking process. I managed with the help of Loomis to get a box opened and to find enough dishes to put on the table, covered with some clean newspapers instead of a damask, and while the candles were getting harder we were softening our hungry appetites by a good cup of coffee, the last of a canister of ground coffee put into my lunch bag by my good mother when I left home; also the last of a little bag of sugar from the same careful provider. Loomis had slipped down to Jesse's and brought a tin cup of Peggy's cream, and with the fried pork and roasted potatoes, some bread we had brought from St. Louis, and the butter that the boys had "shuck" from the "strippings," we had a meal most refreshing, however homely.

Before leaving home your grandfather put up a box for me, of such things as would be comfortable and proper in a log house. There were three bed ticks with bolster and pillow ticks to match, ready to be filled, the feathers sent in a bale by themselves. I had also bedding, a roll of common carpeting, table and bed linen sufficient for a beginning, a set of waiters, knives and forks, and our housekeeping conveniences, which together with my winter clothing and, indeed, all that I had excepting what I brought with me on my seven weeks' trip over the mountains, we had shipped in October, two weeks before we started ourselves, and expected to find them at St. Louis on our arrival there. But what was our disappointment at finding that the boat on which they had been shipped from New Orleans had not been heard from. So I not only found myself lacking in household goods, but minus my winter garments. So I had bought for myself a brown bombazine dress, and some blue and white domestic check to make a morning dress for my log

establishment, and with the help and advice of
the Misses Paddock, had fitted and made them.

On inquiring the price of furniture we found
it extremely high, and hoping, what then
appeared to be hopeless, that I might get the
box which had been sent, felt unwilling to buy
anything it contained that I could possibly do
without. Fortunately we heard of a Mrs.
Bright who had lost her husband and was selling off her furniture preparatory to returning
to Philadelphia. Hither we repaired, and
bought two cherry tables that matched, and
formed a dining table with circular ends.
Here we bought a large bedstead with feather
bed, bolster, and pillows, a small washstand, and
looking-glass for our bedroom, a work table,
and six chairs. As we were leaving the house,
Mrs. Bright, pointing to a large basket she had
packed to be sold at auction, said the articles
contained could not be bought for ten dollars,
but she did not expect they would bring much.
Without looking at the things, we offered her
five dollars, which quite pleased her and was
a fortunate purchase for us. I saw on the top a
knife basket and something that looked like
knives and forks, and so thought it best to secure
the basket and save the expense of these need-
fuls. I bought in St. Louis, also, a piece of
furniture patch, some domestic cotton for a comfortable, a blue dining-set, and a china tea-set ;
was about to buy some table-cloths, but found
that such table linen as could be purchased in

Massachusetts for seventy-five cents a yard was selling in St. Louis for three dollars; so I hoped again for my box and concluded to wait —a tale to be told about the table-cloth.

To go back to the first night spent under our own roof, I recollect that the candles became hard enough to be pulled from the moulds. Four large nails with their points driven into a square block of wood served as one candlestick, the other was supplied by paper being wound around the candle and then inserted into the neck of a glass bottle; this made quite a display. When our neighbor had departed and we had lighted up for the evening we all owned up to feeling very tired; so after getting Simpson's mattress spread on the bed-room floor, with all the loose coverings of old shawls and clothes we could muster, we resigned Joicy to her rest. Two buffalo robes spread on the floor — where a few hours before had stood the work-bench, and between which Loomis and Robert packed themselves with their coats for pillows — finished up our sleeping arrangements.

The next morning we commenced unpacking; do not remember much about it; only how rich I felt when I descended into the depths of Mrs. Bright's clothes basket, where I found knives and forks, iron spoons, two nice sauce-pans, graters, baking tins, spittoons, and many other things that came in play and were useful. Before night we had another bedstead put up for Robert and Loomis, and the old cot set up in the loft for Joicy. Hired a bed and quilt from Mr. Rountree, with whom we had expected to board. When we sent for the bed we found they had been blessed with a son, which explained their hasty retreat from our dwelling.

A few years later I was present at the christening of the children by a Methodist minister; the ceremony was performed at their own home. Their names were Hiram Hawkins Rountree, Aaron Hubbard Rountree, Emily Alfine Hawkins Rountree—who afterwards married Mr. Shumway—was the mother of Hiram, who married Ellen Holmes. They had also a John, with two or three other names attached.

Mr. Rountree was a man of education, and in the earlier times in Illinois was considered a great linguist. Mrs. Rountree was a woman of excellent common sense, a good Christian, and of a most amiable temper; might have taken a higher stand in society had she been educated.

One day there had been some goods brought from St. Louis, a part of which were for Mr. Rountree; he came for them and your father was out. He seemed disappointed that he could not know the amount that had been paid for them, and although not ready to settle the bill, would like to know the cost. I looked and found the bill of the St. Louis merchant, which was receipted. He perused it approvingly, and then in a patronizing manner, asked "if I knew where Mr. Tillson kept his account book? Would I bring it to him; he would make the charge." I found the book and asked him for the bill, which quite puzzled him, and he again repeated what he wanted to do, but I, as if to save him the trouble, commenced making the charges myself. He looked with blank amazement at my performance. At last when he could bear it no longer he jumped up and looking over my shoulder, said, "Why I had no idea you were such a scribe,"—my scribbling then being somewhat better than my pencilings now—"and you have made the charges correctly."

I had some ambition to show off a little, being aware that the "white folks," though very friendly when I met them, were much perplexed to know what Tillson's wife found to do. She didn't spin nor weave, and had that little Dutch girl, and the men helped her to milk. They had hearn that she sot up nights to help Tillson write, but that wasn't much, no how; never seed her in the "truck patch;" didn't believe she knowed how to hoe. I have made quite a digression in speaking of Mr. Rountree and family, and in describing them I give the bearing and lordliness of those from slave-holding states. If they had slaves the authority was exercised over them; if not, the wife was the willing slave; perhaps not so much from fear as from want of knowing anything to assert. There would occasionally be one like Mrs. Kilpatrick who could advance her own opinions.

The first few months' housekeeping was made uncomfortable by the Sunday visiting. We had no regular preaching, and with my new beginnings in domestic duties and the evenings — two in each week — which I devoted in copying letters for your father, I found but little time for reading. The eastern mail came in once in two weeks, and your father being postmaster he usually had papers in every mail from all directions, and although they would be weeks in reaching us they brought the latest intelligence from the civilized world and were about all I could find time to read during the week. I tried to have Sunday for books, when I did not go to "preaching," which time, I felt, was spent without profit and instruction, and but for example's sake would have preferred a quiet day at home.

But there were no such Sundays for me. By the time our breakfast was over and our morning work disposed of there would be a tremendous knocking at the door, accompanied by sonorous demands of "who keeps the house?" Sometimes with the knocking would come, "housekeepers within?" sometimes nothing but a loud, drawling, "h-o-u-s-e-k-e-e-p-e-r-s!" and when the door was opened a backwoodsman would walk in with a big baby on his arm, followed by his wife with the youngest in both her arms, would introduce his lady, and let us know they had come for a day's visit; thinking I was "strange ones 'ere," they reckoned they ought to get acquainted. Being few — either male or female — who wore any out-door garments, the women wore their bonnets in the house and added nothing on going out but a little shawl that came about to the bottom of the waist, said waist being a very short one. I suppose, living as they did in cabins without windows and keeping both doors open for the admittance of light — windows and out of doors was all the same to them in respect to warmth — and having come from a more southern climate, they had never learned the necessity of protection from the cold.

I think during the first three months there was rarely a Sunday when we were not called on to entertain some of these families, who came as if to a show, and would go about the house taking up things and ask, "whart's this 'ere fixin?" open the closet and ask how we sold plates. When informed they were not for sale, could not see why we "wanted such a mighty lot," "never seed so many together, reckoned they cost a heap." The most amusing thing would be their remarks at the table, and their petting the children before coming to the table. "Hush up, honey, and be good; see thar, Auntee Tillson is gwine to have dinner right sure. Reckon she'll have some sweetened bread, cake, and all them pretty dishes." When they had satisfied their appetites and taken a final smoke they would make a move to depart, and invite us to go and spend Sunday with them. We would thank them, and say we would go to see them some week day, we did not visit on the Sabbath. We felt we were very fortunate in breaking up the practice without offending them. Of all our Sunday visitors, I think but one ever repeated the visit on that day, and though they were very jealous and suspicious I never knew of any offense being given.

From the first of January until April there was little change. The mail was brought in once in two weeks. The mail carrier would arrive on Monday night about sunset, leave the mail for Montgomery County, and proceed as far as Colonel Seward's on his way to Springfield, that being the northern terminus of the mail route. Our evenings after receiving the mail were the busiest of all others, your father opening and reading his letters while I regaled myself with the three or four weeks' old eastern newspapers. The carrier returned on Thursday for the eastern mail. Your father's business had become quite extensive, and as it was mostly done through correspondence with eastern landholders he received a large amount of letters, and he generally answered as many as was in his power during the two days that the carrier was gone north. He kept a letter-book into which were copied all the letters sent from the office, and the task was sometimes pretty arduous. Your Uncle Robert would commence in the morning and work diligently, but it was impossible to keep up with your father's rapid penmanship, so, as all the letters had to go into one book and I was a fast writer, it became my privilege to wield the pen in the evening. The evenings were long and not unfrequently would we find ourselves among the small hours of Thursday morning ere our last letter was disposed of and our Wednesday evening's work ended.

After we had been about a month at housekeeping Joel Wright, who had been on an exploring trip through the northern part of the state, returned. As his cabin was closed he wanted to stay with us through the winter, or until he could get a family into his house with whom he could board; so we took him in. We then had heard nothing of our bedding sent by way of New Orleans, but were weekly hoping that we should. So as we were not abundantly supplied, I undertook the business of making a comfortable. For the outside I had the material, but where, O where, was the cotton to be found! I knew everybody had their "cotton patches" and raised their own cotton, but in trying to buy, found that they only picked it from the seed in small quantities. While I was puzzling myself what to do, Mr. Wright brought from his farm some twenty pounds of cotton in the seed; when separated, two-thirds would be seed and the remaining third cotton. I then commenced the arduous task of separating the cotton from the seed, and after much labor and wear and tear of fingers I succeeded in getting enough to fill a comfortable. It had to be carded and made into bats before it could be used, and fortunately my maid-of-all-work knew how to card. But the cards: where were they to be found? After much inquiry I heard of some one who was willing to lend her "kairds" to a Yankee woman. So the cotton was carded, after about a week's labor by Joicy, and meanwhile Loomis had made a quilting frame and the great affair of making a comfortable was accomplished. The neighbors came in to see it. They had "heirn" that Tillson's wife had borrowed kairds, "but reckoned she did'nt know how to spin a draw," and "couldn't think what she could do with kairds."

March at last came after a cheerless winter, and with it the news that our boxes and packages were at the mouth of the Ohio River, where they had been lying all winter while the boat on which they were shipped had been undergoing repairs. Another thing to relieve the monotony was the commencement of an addition to our log house, to consist of two rooms—a parlor and bedroom. They were to be framed, and joined to the log house on the north. We also had our kitchen chimney built and a small window put in, so that in April we moved our cooking utensils into the new establishment. It stood about five feet from the main house and a roof extended across, making a shelter from sun and rain; a platform to pass over was also made. The "white folks" thought we had a "power of room," and were "power down well fixed."

Just before we were ready for the occupancy of the kitchen, our Joicy thought she must go back to St. Louis. She liked to live with us. We had been "right good" to her, she said, but she never lived in one place but a few weeks before. She moaned—longed for a change. Poor Joicy! she could not read, but was of high blood and bearing; said her mother was a cousin of Henry Clay's, and when she married Tarley, Joicy's father, who was a drinker, her relations did not own her and her father kept getting poorer-poorer, and the children got no "larnin." She had a pretty face. Her wardrobe consisted, besides shoes and stockings, of a green flannel petticoat, a calico dress, a white dress, and a checked apron, in all four pieces. When she came from St. Louis she wore her white dress over her calico, which was not in good taste; the stripes and figures of the calico showing unbecomingly through the thin texture of the white cambric; but when, about once a week, she would drop her calico to be washed, and put on her white over her green skirt, with no lining above her waist but what nature had provided, and then to see her sit down on the floor with her lap full of potatoes and turnips and peal them for cooking, with the green shading of her dress below and the pinkie development above, she presented a picture I cannot describe.

So in April I found myself mistress of all work, with our family of four getting on quite systematically. In order to secure Loomis for our building purposes we were obliged to make him one of our family, and it was only by dint of close management that we could keep him at his work. There were so few carpenters in the country that every one who wanted a door for his cabin would come to Loomis, and he would always promise to do their work for them. Poor Loomis, he was good-natured and could not say no to any request, and while we were waiting with impatience at the slow progress of our house, we had to shut our eyes to the little affairs such as shelves or window sash that were being made for some "Sucker's" cabin. If we offended him our last chance for a workman would be at an end; and we had to see the building materials that had been brought sixty miles for our house appropriated to the use of others. Loomis had a weakness for military promotion and was eager to secure the good will of the settlers. His efforts were crowned with success when the next year he was commissioned Major William Loomis. It was more honor than his poor, weak humanity could bear, and while he expanded our work lagged, but there was nothing but patience and endurance for our deliverance.

For about two months I had no servant and Loomis used to get up and make a rousing fire, draw a bucket of cold water from the deep well, and Robert would go out and milk the two cows while I prepared the breakfast, and though it is but my own humble opinion, I think the cabin was as cleanly and orderly as any other that came within my inspection. I used to have black Eda come every week to do my washing, which she would stay and finish up unless she "felt a hurtin' in head," or "mightily like ager," and then she would leave her clothes in tubs and go "hum," the finishing and cleaning up falling to my share.

In April your father went to Vandalia and on his return brought a little Dutch girl, the best thing, he said, that he could find, and Oh! thought I. But to the girl. She rode on the horse behind your father. She had on a German blue calico dress, with a handkerchief tied over her head and another hung on her arm, in which was her wardrobe. They arrived about noon, under a scorching sun. She had light—nearly white—hair, with large, goggle, black eyes, while her skin was as fair as an infant's; the ride, however, of twenty-eight miles under a hot sun and without a bonnet had changed her face from white to red, which, with her startling eyes, gave her a somewhat terrific appearance. She said she was "dur-deen'' (thirteen) years old, and could do a heaper of work before she had the agy; said she had a big agy cake — enlargement of the liver — but could vork most uls well as ever. From her size I should not have thought her more than ten years old. I gave her some dinner, and then sent her to bed to get rested, trusting to the future to see whether I really had ''help,'' or more to take care of. The poor thing, when rested, took hold of work with a cheerful willingness, and with such perfect neatness and faithfulness that I felt I had in her a treasure.

About this time came court week, the first court that had been held, after my arrival. After breakfast, as your father was starting for the court house, two miles distant, he told me he should invite Starr and Mills home to dinner, and having the addition of a Baptist minister from Maine, who had quartered himself upon us, I had the table set for eight, with ample provisions for that number. But what was my astonishment when instead of the two invited guests they kept up the cavalcade until fourteen had dismounted in front of the house. Someone had told them that we were to dine the court that day, and without waiting for an invitation they pushed on, as hungry men would instinctively do. The first thing for me was to repair to the kitchen and put Doris in the way of preparing a dish of ham and eggs. Then, in the presence of all the bar, with Doris' help I lengthened the table, and with much planning and squeezing succeeded in getting their honors around the board. The chickens, which would have been all-satisfying on my first table, dwindled into insignificance on my lengthened board. The vegetables were dealt out sparingly, but thanks to ham and eggs my distinguished guests seemed full and happy. My poor pot pudding I had made with such care and satisfaction, and the exquisite sauce, its accompaniment, was most sparingly divided, much to my mystification. There was some consolation in perceiving that some of the gentlemen had discovered the mistake of intention, and were not a little mortified at their position.

The court-week entertainment brings to mind another personage, the "down east" Baptist preacher who came to us one Saturday afternoon, tired and jaded, his business being to inquire about a section of land. Your father invited him to stay until Monday, much to my inconvenience, as I could not think for some time how or where I should deposit him for the night. But being decent looking, and professing Godliness—two things which did not abound in our neighborhood—I felt disposed to extend whatever hospitality I could. On Sunday he went with us to the Hard-shell Baptist meeting, and was invited to preach. Comparing him with Father Street, he was quite an orator, though I had a wicked feeling that he had a better capacity for committing and repeating other ministers' sermons than for composing himself. Monday he was sick, threatened with ague, continued to grow sicker; and while I was hoping and watching for his departure, your father informed me that Plummer was a carpenter by trade, had followed that calling until called to preach the Gospel; that he had proposed to remain a while and do some carpenter work that we were needing, and he had agreed to employ him. O dear! thought I, what can I do? but as the bargain was completed, I, of course, had nothing to do but acquiesce. A gleam of hope came in to take off some of the disagreeable in thinking that our rooms, of which we were sadly in want, might thus be finished by September. Judge of my chagrin when your father told me that Plummer had been telling him of a new cheese-press that would work admirably, and as we were milking seven cows it was a pity not to have a dairy. Your father seemed quite elated with the plan. He knew nothing of the outlay for the utensils needed in cheese-making, nor the labor it would bring upon me. I had no other help than little Doris, who, poor thing! would work until after she had washed her dinner dishes and made her kitchen quite clean, and then get into her cot, rolling herself up like a caterpillar, and asking me to "woke me up 'ginst supper time comes."

About this time William Porter came to us

sick, having chills and fever every other day. Our family then consisted—besides your father, Uncle Robert, and myself—of Loomis, Porter, Plummer, and Horn, who worked on the farm; six hungry men to be fed three times a day; besides which your father had told all but Porter that they could have their washing done in the house, and my compassion for Porter—who was of another style from the rest—constrained me to take care of him. Plummer, besides his mechanical skill and clerical accomplishments, professed great taste in gardening; he had brought some seeds from New England and as a matter of favor had planted them in our garden. When he asked your father to go out and look at the growth of his plants—and which meant besides to hear a long horticultural discourse—he would be turned over to me, as it was something that interested women more than men. Plummer had a fondness for inviting company, and would ask the youngest of the settlement to come to see him. On such occasions, as also when we had any company, he would ascend to the loft (his dormitory) and doffing his carpenter's garb, come down with a gown on, and preside with all the dignity of a bishop. Every day he grew more and more odious to me; I expressed it to your father, who admitted that he was disagreeable, but exhorted me to better discipline my feelings and not be annoyed by 'what I could not remedy.

One day your father came home with a most woeful tale which was in circulation in the settlement, and thought we had better send him away. I had long considered him a weak-minded, conceited fop, and his religion put on. As I was less prone then than now to show respect where I could not feel it and not so to smother contempt when disgusted, the parson had long perceived that I at least did not reverence him, however dull his perceptive powers were in other directions. Your father did not tell him the cause of his dismissal, but that as our family was large it would not be convenient for him to remain longer, at which his ire was kindled and he said he saw where the shoe pinched, throwing all the responsibility and blame on me.

About that time James Black (afterwards Colonel Black) sent us word that he was sick, and should die unless he could get out of Vandalia, another matter of duty before us, but lest he should die and his life be required at our hands, we sent for him to come. Our family was made much pleasanter by the exchange of guests. Our neighbor S., who hated Black and Porter next to the Tillsons, made himself busy in making low and vulgar remarks about our keeping those lazy drones about us.

The last of August had come; our chimney of logs had been removed to make way for one of brick, which was to serve for both the new frame and the log part of the house.

There had been a contract for bricks; they were to be delivered on the first of September; a man in Greenville was to furnish them. Think of our consternation when, at the time he was to deliver them, he coolly let us know that he had given up brick-making, and there were none to be obtained within forty miles. There was but one alternative, viz: to get brickmakers and have a brickyard made at the bottom of our garden, which was speedily commenced and rapidly pushed forward. All the men having to be fed at our table, we could do no other way.

Saturday, September 14, 1823, Bird, the head brickman, pronounced the bricks sufficiently baked, nothing but to have them cool enough to handle, and then a new chimney to be commenced, a bright and cheering announcement. A silver lining from under the dark cloud that had overshadowed me, I with a light heart went to work, and with the aid of Doris accomplished wonders in the cake and pie line, Doris occasionally reminding me that it was Saturday and that the kitchen would need "a helper;" heap of cleaning, and that heper tins to scrub, and "heper oder tings to do first we make supper." My work accomplished, I left Doris to her loved task of polishing every tin, and making clean every inch of the little log kitchen, and putting things in order for God's day, as she called the Sabbath. Her health had greatly improved, and with it her usefulness.

Our family was now reduced to six, Loomis having gone to perform some of his promised labor, and Mr. Black had been invited to spend a week in the Rev. Jesse Townsend's family, much to my relief. Just before tea time W. H. Brown, who with his wife had been passing the summer at her father's, rode up, with Harriet behind him, on horseback. There was to be a "big meeting" in Bond County.

It was then the practice in the Presbyterian church, while the country was so sparsely settled, to have at each communion a two days' meeting commencing on Friday night and continuing through the Sabbath. Ministers from different parts of the country were present, and to the Gospel-loving portion it was a profitable season. To the young girls and boys, a display of their best garments was perhaps the absorbing weakness; but the unscrupulousness of the politicians, who attended these meetings with no other motive than the purpose of electioneering for themselves or their friends, was not to my taste. Mr. Brown had brought his wife to stay with me, while he with your father would go to the Lauthlin settlement, sixteen miles distant, to attend the meeting. Mr. Brown was not *then* a Christian man, but was led by politics and worldly gain; still, he looked quite satisfied when he told your father he would like to go with him to the big meeting. Judge Enos, who had been to Washington and had been appointed receiver of public moneys for the Sangamon

District, and was returning by way of Montgomery to take Wm. Porter as his clerk, also came. Porter had been sick, and for several months had no other home than ours, and without the means of paying for a dose of medicine. We had become much interested in him, and although the arrival of another guest sadly interfered with my limited arrangements, yet the prospect for him was so encouraging that I went with a light heart to the loft, where I prepared a cleanly bed for the Judge on one of the rude bedsteads; the other was left for Robert and Porter, and another made on the floor for brickmaker Bird.

After our guests had retired for the night and we were about to lie down a loud thumping came at the kitchen door, and Loomis' voice demanding admittance, with Doris' persistent refusal to let him in, arrested our attention. Your father went to the door and found his neighbor, Joel Wright, holding by the mane a sick horse, while he and Loomis each had a bundle of herbs. I had been feeling a relief from the absence of Loomis that evening, both on account of his uncontrollable loquacity, as well as being spared from witnessing the sad havoc that would have come upon my pies. Lest you may think me unduly careful of my pies, I will try at some other time to give you the particulars of my first pumpkin-pie baking. It seems Loomis had gone to spend the night with Wright, and finding Wright's horse sick

had prescribed a decoction of prairie herbs,
and proposed to Wright to come to our kitchen
and boil the same, telling him that he would
find everything there convenient for their use.
Your father, of course, bade them welcome to
the kitchen and all that was in it, referring
them to Doris for whatever they might need.
Doris, who was always telling how "plasum
and lafum"—pleasant and laughing—Mr.
Tillson was, stoutly remonstrated against having
the herbs being brought on her clean floor,
and the boiler, that we would need for washing on Monday, made filthy from the boiling
of the weeds, and her tin dippers and pans
used which she had just polished and displayed
each on its own particular nail on the kitchen
wall. Besides, there would be "heper" folks
to get breakfast for, and tomorrow was God's
day; "God's book say not to work on that
day." But permission had been given, and the
work commenced. I found myself too sick and
tired from Saturday's effort to sleep, so I got
up and sat by my little window, opposite the
kitchen door, so near that I was obliged to be
the hearer of more than I could wish. As the
morning was chilly, and but one fire-place on
the premises, I repaired early to the kitchen
and with Doris put things to rights again, and
had breakfast in progress before any of the
guests came to the door to ask permission to
put their feet to the fire. Judge Enos first put
his head in and asked to be admitted to the

culinaries, and one after another until the dining room was quite deserted.

After breakfast Judge Enos and Porter started for Springfield, Mr. Brown and Mr. Tillson for the Bond County meeting, leaving Mrs. Brown and myself alone. Before the next morning we had another visitor. Our dear Charley opened his eyes upon the rough cabin walls, and with his chubby fists in his mouth he looked—as Mother Kilpatrick declared—as if he was two months old and knew us all. We felt we had a precious gift, but the way to take care of it was the puzzle. It was the fifteenth of September, the nights cool and chilly, and the days too cool to expose a thing so tender to the rough blasts. We had a sheet-iron stove set in the wall between the bed-rooms; when the wind favored, we could kindle a fire to dress the baby, but when adverse winds prevailed we had him rolled in a blanket and taken to the kitchen to be dressed. The toilet was soon made, as the western women felt that water was a deadly application for babies. They kept their babies' heads covered with a thick calico cap until they were several months old, in which time a black surface would form and cover the scalp. They would then commence a season of cleaning by saturating the head with either hog or "bar's" (bear) grease, and then as it would come loose, pick off the black coating. As it would usually come off in large blotches, it gave a sad, leopard-like appearance to the little "honey."

Mrs. Kilpatrick offered her services as nurse and stayed with me two weeks, and rendered all the assistance that she knew and felt to be necessary, and did many things that I have no doubt she deemed unnecessary. She asked me the first morning, after I had taken a cup of coffee with some light bread crumbled into it, what she should get for my dinner; had heard the Yankee women dieted at such times; for herself, she always took pork and cabbage for her first meal. I mention this to show her ideas of nursing the sick, which extended into all her other ways of management; yet she was kind, and probably exercised much forbearance in gratifying the notions of a Yankee.

During the time she was with me the chimney had been built, Mr. Black had returned from the Townsends, and I, with a baby two weeks old, was again reinstated at my family's head, said family consisting of five men, and with no other help than poor little Doris. After about a week I began to give out, and your father went around the settlement until he found a girl. I asked her what she could do. She said she "tuck keer of the truck patch in summer, and milked the cows and spinned right smart in winter." I asked her how old she was. "I'se older nor I'se good," was the reply. I found very few parents or children knew their ages. She said her mother thought she could "yearn" six bits a week at spinning, and she must have that for house-work. She could milk "right smart," and bring in wood, make fires, and some few things to make Doris' work a little easier, but on the whole we felt relieved when at the end of two weeks she went back to her mammy. I did not hear of her again until some ten years afterwards, when there was a great scarcity of eggs and the farmers were saving all they could for the St. Louis market. As I was about to give Bela White and Miss Stratton a wedding entertainment, I dispatched a lad through the country to get eggs for my wedding cake. He had but little success until he came to Forehand's, and was there refused, but when on leaving Mrs. Forehand found out it was for me he wanted them she called him back and said "that ever since her Jane lived with us she had allus meaned to do us some gud. She allus thought a scandalous heap on Tillson's wife, and she would send me some eggs if Jarvis —her husband—didn't like it." With the strong feeling that prevailed among the poor whites at that time against the Yankees, I could never understand how it was that we lived so peaceably among them, and with all the trials of being in such a community we had the confidence and good will of most of them, which were manifested in various ways.

Jesse Buzan—who rented our bottom-field —had a wife whose great enjoyment seemed to consist in coming every day to inspect. She was taken quite by surprise when one day I offered her a piece of what I told her was Yankee pie. She looked blank and said, "I didn't think you would say the like of that; I allus knowed youens were all Yankees, but Billy said 'don't let on that we know it, kase it'll jest make them mad.'" I told her I was proud to be called a Yankee, and that she need never fear to speak of it. She looked incredulous, and then said, "Billy and I have always found you jess so, but some folks say they have been here when Yankees come in, and you talk a heap of things that you don't say to us." "Do they say I talk against anyone?" "O no, not that; but you use a heap of words to Yankees that you don't when you talk to us. They say, too, you put a lot of nasty truck in your bread. It is what you keep in a bottle, purlass, I believe, is the name, and they say it is full of dead flies, and bugs, and cricket legs." I brought forward my little bottle of dissolved pearl ash, looking so clear and pure, and showed it to her, but it seemed hard to give up her old prejudice.

November 16, 1871.

I have not, as I hoped to do, been able to write much of late, and find that what I have written only brings me a year into my western experience, and will in future try to avoid prosiness and state things as they suggest themselves. We lived on in the usual way until the July of 1824, when our new parlor and a sleeping-room above was so far finished as to admit of occupancy, and was meekly furnished to serve the demands of comfort and to avoid the censure and envy of the multitude.

After we had settled ourselves again a little more comfortable as to house accommodations, your father suggested the plan of opening a small store, to bring from St. Louis such goods as the natives were needing and to take in exchange butter, honey, beeswax, maple sugar, and such things as they could raise. He thought it would be a convenience and benefit to the neighborhood; but his strongest inducement was to get up something that would interest his brother. Robert did not like the business in his office as he had hoped, and did not feel interested in farming. He thought there was a clerkship in a store at Halifax he could get, and wanted to go back. Your father did not want him to return dissatisfied; nor did he feel that it would be the best move for him, and as a matter of encouragement proposed the store to Robert and suggested to me that we should give up our two little bedrooms and use our new room, our parlor, as a bedroom until we could build another. It was a sad inconvenience to me, but I believe I did not object, and tried to make things go as well as the nature of the case would permit. Robert seemed to enjoy the preparation, and was quite busy in making arrangements for receiving and packing the butter for a few months, but finally it lost its charm and homesickness again took possession of his mind, and when customers came I found it easier to go in and wait upon them than to look for and find Robert. So I had quite an experience in mercantile life, and in keeping accounts with the Suckers.

The next year, the winter of 1824, the brick house at the county seat—Hillsboro—was commenced, and our arrangements made for renting the farm. The house was to be built by contract—a one-story brick house. The reason of our giving up our abode at the farm, where your father had expected to remain, was a dispute that had been going on between Colonel Seward and the county commissioners about the county seat. It had been located on the west side of Shoal Creek, adjoining Colonel Seward's farm, and but a mile from our house, and had been named Hamilton, after Hamilton, Ohio, Colonel Seward's former place of residence. Things worked smoothly for a while, until the misunderstanding with the Colonel. Then there was a petition to the legislature and a new location. The county seat was changed from the east to the west side of the creek. Your father, being postmaster, was obliged to move the post office to the county seat. Mr. Rountree, who was clerk of court, was obliged to keep his office there also; so he—Mr. Rountree—put up a small log cabin for his office and your father made him deputy post-master, to deliver letters between the arrival of the mails. Not far from that time the mails began to arrive once a week, and it was only necessary for your father to be there and receive them and make them up to be sent away.

It was nearly two miles from our house, however, to the office, and in winter the creek would be so flooded that it was almost impossible for him to cross. Indeed, it was a dangerous performance at best. One night the mail had been delayed by high waters between Vandalia and Hillsboro, and he had to cross the creek in the dark, with the water coming up to the saddle. He came home completely drenched. After he had got himself into dry clothing and eaten his supper, he told me that he had that day seen Dickerson,[17] of Vandalia, and had employed him to put up a brick building that would serve for an office, store, and post office. The building was to have two rooms. I told him if he would put up four rooms instead of two I would take the baby and go there to live, for I was tired of the danger to which he was exposed in crossing that creek at all times of the night and in all stages of water.

I spoke from the impulse of my feelings at

[17] According to W. H. Perrin's History of *Bond and Montgomery Counties* (Chicago, 1882), the builder of Tillson's house was one John Nickerson.

the time, not thinking that anything would ever come from it. He sat and looked in the fire for about half an hour, then went to his desk, brought a sheet of paper, took another himself, and said: "I have been thinking over what you said about moving into town, and now I will draw a plan of a house and you may draw another and we will compare and decide on what kind of a building to put up. So we both went to work, and each drew a plan, and then compared and changed and settled upon what both thought would be about right, and before we went to bed had the business all decided, a thing that neither of us had thought of three hours before.

I will give you a drawing, showing the plan of the first brick house ever built in Montgomery County, or within twenty miles of it. This was the winter of 1824–25. Dickerson commenced his brickyard in the early spring of '25, and promised a house ready for occupancy by the spring following, '26; but alas for promises. Dickerson was a smart business man, a gentlemanly fellow, but by some mischance he was owing more than he had the means of paying, and your father was obliged to take a bill of sale of all the bricks that were being made lest Dickerson's creditors should claim them, and thereby we should lose our house. The original plan was for a one-story cottage. Your father came in one day and asked if I would object to having it made two stories, giving as a reason that he had already advanced more for Dickerson's debts than would cover the expense of a one-story house. The thing seemed so formidable that it was quite an alarm. A two-story brick house among the log cabins, it would never do. What would the natives say? And how should I feel to have the care of such a mansion? But the thing was decided upon and your father seemed wonderfully pleased.

In October of 1825 another noble boy was given us. I had occupied my parlor for a bedroom, and John was much more comfortably housed and lodged than was his elder brother, who was two years his senior. I had made the acquaintance of Mrs. Townsend, who was with me and remained until John was a week old. She had Julia—afterwards Mrs. Hinckley—with her. There was but three days difference in the ages of Charley and Julia, and the new baby was to them a most wonderful event. Julia said he was her "bubber," and she would have him to help "Pater Willie make tacks"—hay stacks. Charley would get angry and cry, because if Pater Willie had booboo Don, he would have no bubber. When Mrs. Townsend went home, Rosetta—Eliza Braley's mother—came and spent the winter with me. She was only thirteen years old, but until I could get out of my room was the only housekeeper I had. I had old Black Lucy in the kitchen, but she could do nothing out of it.

She could cook her three meals and bring them into the dining room, and do the family washing. Whatever else was done had to be done by Rosetta or myself, as I gained strength to go about, but there was more left undone than done for awhile.

The next year, the October of 1826, I had promised Caleb and Lucy a vacation, or, as the negroes called it, a "long broad," their term for a long visit. The time I had arranged for their "broad" was when your father and Uncle Robert were to be absent, and I expected to have no family but myself and the two children and a Miss Seymour, who had a few months before come into the settlement. She was a homesick girl; had come from North Carolina with her brother's family and her father, who was an old, broken down Irish gentleman, a devout Christian, and of higher cultivation than his children. We had besides Caleb and Lucy a white boy, who was indispensable to me as a house servant.

Your father had been very busy for several days preparing papers which he was to send off by your Uncle Robert to Vandalia, and after he left was getting ready to go to Edwardsville to act as one of the commissioners for the closing up of the old bank at that place, but was suddenly taken ill, and the morning he was to leave found him in bed with a raging fever and a delirium which was truly distressing. He imagined the fringes on the window curtains were rattlesnakes, and imagined it to be my duty to keep them from the bed. Miss Seymour had a boil on her foot and could not wear a shoe, and instead of being a help was a decided bother. Her foot being first and foremost, and indeed all she could talk about, I found myself in *one* of the tight places, not *the* tight place, for I found too many such. Besides my performances in the kitchen as cook, and attendance on all the "Suckers" that came to the store, measuring cotton cloth and linsey, weighing coffee, indigo, and madder — or as they called it, mather — and in exchange for which would be the weighing of butter, beeswax, honey, and counting of eggs; chickens they sold by the "par" (pair).

When my mercantile labor was ended, and I released from my duties behind the counter, it would be quite a circumstance not to find my year-old baby crying for mamma, or my three-year-old boy up to his elbow in mischief, or something burnt in the kitchen; for Willis, our boy, though indispensable in my housekeeping, was but an eye-servant, and as outdoor occupations were more in accordance with his taste, would find himself under the necessity of canvassing the hay-mow for eggs or feeding the chickens while the things left in his care in the kitchen would be most sadly charred. The customers gone, the babies peaceful, Willis called in, the hens driven out of the kitchen, with time only to hear a passing

remark from Sarah as to the condition of her
"fut" (foot), and then I was ready to assume
the duties of nurse, your father expressing his
surprise that I would stay away so long and
trying to impress me with the importance of
staying in the room lest he might want something in my absence, and a solemn charge to
keep Sarah and the children out of the room.

One day he seemed more comfortable, and
told me that I must write some letters that
should be sent away the next morning. So
after giving Sarah a charge to watch Willis
and see that he took care of the children, and
that he did not run off to the stable or leave
the kitchen door open to the occupancy of the
hens or pigs, I gathered my writing material
and repaired to the bed side, where I was to
act as amanuensis. I at first had to write to
each bank commissioner, stating his sickness
and inability to be with them; then a long letter
to Stephen B. Munn of New York, and also
some others. The writing finished, I had to
send Willis to the office with the letters to be
mailed. He returned, bringing back the letters,
and informed me that Mr. Rountree was away
and that "Mrs. Rountree did not know nothing,
no how, about postoffice." Your father then
sent back to the office, two miles, to have all
the letters brought to him that had been put
in the office the previous week, and to me was
assigned the task of making up the mail. It
was no small task, either, for as he had for-

gotten to send for the way-bills — which are printed blanks to be filled out and put with each package — I had to make out the whole thing, way-bills and all, in regular postoffice order. After a few days your Uncle Robert returned and we immediately sent him to Greenville for a physician; it being twenty miles, it was an all-day's ride. I had not sent before because Dr. Newhall, our family physician, was not in Greenville, and your father did not profess confidence in any other, so I had to carry him through a course of treatment the best I could, though with fearful forebodings as to whether I was pursuing the right course. The anxiety and responsibility I felt about his sickness was more than all the labor and care with which I was burdened.

After he had consented to have a doctor, and Robert had returned with Dr. Drake and he had approved of my treatment, I felt wonderfully relieved; a heavy responsibility had been lifted from my poor, tired-out body and mind. The doctor stayed two days and watched the progress of his convalescence, and then said he must go home, as he had other patients requiring his care. Your father remonstrated stoutly against his leaving, and it was with the greatest difficulty he could bring him to any reasonable understanding as to the necessity of his going home. When my mind was more at ease I began to feel how thoroughly worn down and tired I had become, and shall never forget the sensation it gave me to see little Julia's green hood coming through the gate, and holding it open for her mother. To those who have never known the loneliness that had encircled me for the few past weeks, my feelings could not be described. The sight of a face beaming with kindness as was Mother Townsend's when she came in and said, "And why didn't thee let me know?" Such friends and such acts of friendship can never be forgotten, nor can they be understood by those who have not been in like isolation.

Mrs. Townsend spent a week with me, and took John—who was about a year old—to sleep with her and Julia. Ever after his father was taken sick he seemed to have a horror of everybody; would not let Sarah touch him, or do the least thing for him; he seemed to feel that something was wrong, as if a perfect terror had taken hold of him. Through the day he would hold on to the skirts of my dress as I passed from room to room; then at night I had to take him in my arms and lie down on the bed beside your father, and if obliged to get up and wait upon him, John would wake and cling to me with such a frenzied cry that I would be obliged to carry him about in my arms until I could get him quieted enough to lie down. It seemed a wonderful release when I could give him up to Mother Townsend and undress and go to bed at night, a thing I had not done for more than a week. Mrs. Townsend did not leave me until Caleb and Lucy returned; the children were happy and pleased to have them back; and your father getting so as to sit up a little, when we heard that your Uncle Charles was on his way to Illinois.

It had been four years since I left my New England home and in that time I had seen no face that I had ever known before, excepting your father's and Uncle Robert's, and it was with no little exciting interest that I looked forward to his arrival. When I left home he was a lad of eighteen, in a store in Boston. Four years had brought him to be a handsome young man of twenty-two. We had a happy meeting. Charles seemed wonderfully pleased with the children, and they with him; but as they had never seen but one uncle they refused to acknowledge him as such, and would say, "Robert is my uncle."

In speaking of your father's requirements when he was sick, it might seem to those who did not know his kind heart that his was a difficult spirit to contend with. I know not why it is, but have observed it frequently that when a difficult and uproarious case of humanity is prostrated by sickness it becomes gentle and submissive and exhibits a lamb-like spirit. Your father in health was amiable and mild, and had no love for exercising authority over others, but in sickness he understood every duty of a nurse and was faithful in seeing that it was performed. As soon as he was able to attend to business came the preparation for the land sales at Vandalia. The sales were of lands on which the taxes had not been paid. They commenced early in the winter and continued for about two months, a certain number being put up every day and most of them bought in for the amount of the taxes. The lands sold were mostly soldiers' bounty lands, and owned by persons in the eastern states. The yards of land lists that had to be copied before the sales brought another season of hurry, and as I could write then with a better hand than I now do, and quite rapidly, I was called into the business, and our evenings were often prolonged to the morning hours.

After your father started for Vandalia, taking your Uncle Robert with him to assist in his writing, I commenced preparations for my eastern visit, to which I had been looking forward for the last four years, and as the whole preparation for leaving home, providing a home for Caleb and Lucy in our absence, and of getting a comfortable outfit for your father, myself, and the children, devolved upon me, I found myself fully occupied. Mrs. Townsend helped me some, but as her daughter, Rosetta, was to go with us, she had her wardrobe to prepare. Such a thing as hiring a day's sewing was then unheard of in that region. A week before we started eastward our furniture was removed to our new house and packed in one of the rooms. In another room the office furniture was deposited, the office to be kept open, your Uncles Robert and Charles acting as land-agents and store-keepers. We had a cabin built for Caleb and Lucy not far from the new house, and left them with a barrel of flour, corn meal and bacon, and coffee and sugar sufficient for the six months that we expected to be absent.

The day before we left Caleb came to us with one of his sanctimonious faces that he could put on whenever he wanted to carry any point, and after a profound bow and a speech of negro blarney, made known his request that your father would give him something to show that he was a free man; that he wanted to live and die with us and the dear children; but life was onsartain, and we might not live to come back, and then he and Lucy would have to be sold like other niggers.

The law of the state was very hard on those who liberated slaves, requiring them to give bonds for the good behavior of the negro, and should they become chargeable to the state for their support those who had liberated them had to meet the expenses. When Governor Coles went to Illinois, he entered a quarter section of land and took with him all the slaves he had inherited from his father's estate in Virginia and gave them their freedom and a home on the prairie land he had provided for them, but had not given bonds to the state that they should not be chargeable; had intended to do so, but neglected it up to the time he was nominated as a candidate for governor. Party feeling ran very high at that time, and a determination among the southern portion of the inhabitants to have the constitution changed and slavery admitted to the state was carried to a great length. Mr. Coles, who had been born in Virginia and always lived among slaves, had come to the new state of Illinois with an honest intention of taking a decided stand on the side of freedom by giving up nearly all his patrimony, was looked upon by the southern aristocracy as a most bitter foe to their cause, and to retaliate they brought suit against him for non-compliance with the laws of the state and recovered three thousand dollars, but lost their democratic governor, and Coles. Mr. Coles had held a high position in social life, had traveled abroad, been private secretary of President Madison, was a man of fine sensibilities and strictly moral character, but such a man must be put down, and a suit was brought against him and three thousand dollars added to his other expenses in freeing and providing for the poor negroes.

Well, I have made quite a digression from Caleb and Lucy to Governor Coles, but the case was the same with your father, and as Caleb was a dangerous fellow when drunk, and in your father's absence much given to spreeing, it was a case requiring some wisdom. It may be necessary to explain why we were in

possession of slaves. Nothing but dire necessity could have induced us to the course we
pursued in taking them. Caleb and Lucy were
among those brought into Illinois while it was
a territory. When it became a state, the constitution permitted those who held slaves to
retain them as indentured servants, or slaves,
with the privilege of selling their indentures to
others, or to send them down the river and to
sell them for as much as they could get. Their
children were to be the property of the masters
with whom they were born until they were
eighteen or twenty-five years of age, I have
forgotten which, and they then became free
negroes. Caleb and Lucy were the indentured
slaves of Robert McLaughlin of Vandalia.
He was an uncle of Governor Duncan's, and
kept the principal hotel at Vandalia. Your
father always stopped there during the winter,
and would frequently speak of Lucy as a good
cook.

Your father came home from Vandalia at
one time and told me that Mr. McLaughlin[18]

[18] Col. Robert K. McLaughlin was a native of Virginia, a lawyer by profession, who removed first to
Kentucky and shortly thereafter to Belleville, Illinois.
He was elected to the office of state treasurer in 1819
and thereupon removed to Vandalia, the new capital,
which continued to be his home until his death in
1862. A history of Fayette County records that
Colonel McLaughlin had five negroes at Vandalia,
that they soon ran away, and that he made no effort
to recover them. Apparently Mrs. Tillson's account
of this phase of his career is the more accurate one.

asked him to buy out their indentures; said that Lucy was valuable to them, but Caleb was getting old, and quarreled with the other negroes, and unless he could find someone to take them he had made up his mind to send them to New Orleans and sell them. Caleb was sixty years of age and Lucy thirty, and they had about twenty-five years to serve — what should he do? Your father thought that if we could better their condition, and thereby secure Lucy as a cook, it would not be amiss to make the purchase. I had never seen Caleb and Lucy and consequently had none of the sympathy which your father felt for them, and with my persistent feeling against slavery would not consent to the bargain, and no more had been said about it.

One morning, after a night of little rest from the fatigue of overworking the day before, I went into the kitchen to make preparation for breakfast. I had no girl. Nelly, the girl who a few months before took the water to the gentleman's rooms — you have heard the story — had behaved badly and I had sent her off, and I felt a relief when she was gone. When I opened the kitchen door that morning there were two queer specimens of humanity stretched horizontally, covering almost the entire vacant space on our small kitchen floor. When I appeared a black figure arose and drawing his tall proportions into their most graceful attitude and putting on the same patronizing face that he wore when he would say, "I'se not like de rest; I'se half Delaware Ingin; de best blood when cool, but, miza me, when het up de worst blood det eben is in Ingin tribes," he bowed obsequiously and said, "I am Caleb, and dis is Lucy, on de floor. I'se had acquaint'nce with Mr. Tillson for some years; I allers blacks his boots and makes his fires when he's in Vandalia. I'se broke with Master Mac, and I thought I would come and try to git in with you, madam. I'll kindle the fire, and den you can tell Lucy 'bout de breffast." I made my way back to the bedroom and when I returned found Lucy up and awaiting my orders. It was no small consideration with me, worn down as I was, to have someone to cook a comfortable dinner, and at night make some biscuit and get up a supper that pleased your father, without the necessity of being over the big, open fire-place and lifting the Dutch oven myself. Still it was slavery — the price of blood — that haunted me. As there was a penalty attached to those who harbored runaway slaves, your father wrote immediately to Mr. McLaughlin, informing him of our morning surprise and asking him what to do with them.

After about a month Lucy came to the kitchen in great glee and told me that Master Robert was at the gate and was coming in with Mr. Tillson, and she was "gwine tu have some fuss rate biskits, and cook some of dat nice ham, jes' to let de slave folks see dat de Yankees has as good things as theyuns; and please, will you get out some of your best deserves?'' After the table was ready she came again to know if she could roll up the back window curtains in the dining room, so that by going out doors she could look in and see how Old Massa liked his supper. Of course all Lucy's reasonable requests were complied with, and ''Old Massa'' gave evidence of his appreciation of a good meal.

After supper, in the parlor, Mr. McLaughlin and your father proceeded to business. He had made up his mind that if your father would give him five hundred dollars for the time Lucy was to serve, thirty years, and fifty feet of plank from his mill for Caleb's indentures, which were not for as long a time as Lucy's, he would give him a quit-claim to their future services. If not, he should take them to New Orleans, where he could get a higher price, but, professing a kind sympathy for their welfare, would prefer to make the sacrifice. He was to spend the night with us and the proposal was to be decided in the morning. I saw that your father's wish was to retain them, and as my kitchen labors were to be abated, and feeling, too, as he did, that I could not think of having them sent off to the slave pens of New Orleans, we both concluded to keep them. Work was made lighter, but conscience not quite easy.

A Woman's Story

Having brought my reminiscences to the close of the four-and-a-half years of Illinois, I will, before beginning on another year, give a parting retrospect of my isolation while at our log cabin at the farm. In the four years I had left home once, to go to Vandalia, where I spent nearly a week, taking with me Charley, who was six weeks old. We also took Mr. Black, who had been sick and with us for the four previous months, but had so far recovered as to be able to enter the auditor's office as clerk for Colonel Berry.[19] About a year afterwards I went to Greenville and spent two days with the Blanchards'. The third year of my backwoods life I went to St. Louis, stopping at Collinsville and spending the Sabbath at Deacon Collins'.

That Sunday was communion day, and I there met Mrs. Breath, who with her son Edward for a driver had come down from the Marine settlement in a wagon, drawn by two stout oxen. Ed., the teamster, was afterwards the beloved missionary to Persia, and Mrs. Breath did not feel her dignity lowered or any apology necessary on account of her rude turnout, but simply remarked that they had lost their horses. I also met with Mrs. B——, from St. Louis, who was a visitor there. I saw her in

[19] Elijah C. Berry of Kaskaskia, first state auditor of Illinois.

St. Louis when I made my first visit, and when I had all my nice wedding wardrobe, and was complimented on my good taste in dressing. "Like begets like," and I was not aware that two and a half years with such coarse surroundings had told so heavily on my personal appearance. Mrs. B. somewhat officiously tried to convince me of the fact, saying I dressed old enough for a lady of old Mrs. Collins' age. I had had an attack of intermittent fever the autumn previous and lost my hair, so that I had been under the necessity of wearing a cap, and as there had been no style to follow I made rather an outlandish appearance; I had taken one of my best collars, put on a muslin crown, and trimmed it with lace, a thing that in comparison with the checkered cotton handerkerchiefs worn on the heads of our native women was quite a triumph, but when I showed my head to the St. Louis aristocracy I felt decidedly night-cappy. Arriving at St. Louis the Paddocks gave me hints and lectures on the same subject; was there three or four days and brushed up a little. Started for Edwardsville; on our way homeward spent two days at Major Hopkins'. The last night I spent there Charley was taken sick, and in the morning the whole family remonstrated about our leaving with so sick a child.

The flies, which at that season swarmed on the prairie, made it dangerous to attempt crossing in the daytime, as they would attack horses in such a way as to make them perfectly frantic and unmanageable. This was another reason urged why it would be unsafe for us to start, but your father had a business engagement to meet and his mind was made up; so taking a bottle of something to allay Charley's thirst, for he had a high fever, and taking him on my lap, we started on our ride of forty miles. There was a strong wind that day which was fortunate for us as the flies could not settle on the horses as in a calm, and by a most furious driving, which your father well understood, we were enabled to reach home before night.

These three visits were all that I made out of our own neighborhood for the first four-and-a-half years. Twice in that time I spent a day at ''Parson Townsend's,'' seven miles from us. I spent one day at Colonel Seward's, one at Butler Seward's, and occasionally would ride up to ''Father Townsend's'' and spend a day or part of a day. Among the western neighbors, I dined twice at Esquire Kilpatrick's, in the cabin without a floor; once at Jesse Buzan's, once at Commodore Yoakum's, which, with the exception of one wedding, and one ''infare,'' covered all my absences from the old home.

Perhaps you do not understand the word ''infare.'' It is the reception of the bridal pair and other invited guests at the house of the groom's father the day after the marriage. It was the only time I ever witnessed the western custom of riding for the bride's bottle.

If I had not already gone into so many particulars, I would give you a description of the race. The wedding I attended was that of Mrs. Kilpatrick's daughter, who was married to a stranger who had recently appeared in the neighborhood calling himself a doctor. I knew as soon as I put my eye on him that he was a scamp, but for Mrs. Kilpatrick's sake I invited them all to dine with me the next day.

The story of my visits could soon be told; but visitors and hangers-on were legion. When preparing breakfast I never knew whether it was for my own family, or several more. The "bounty-landers," who were on their way from the military tract to Vandalia, would, after spending the night at Colonel Seward's, get on in the morning as far as the land-office, of course arriving just in time for breakfast. Besides which all the ministers made our house their depot. If we chanced to be patronized by a well-informed and good man, we felt it a favor conferred, but I am sorry to say the greater number of the clerical brothers were poor pay. Sarah Seymour spent about six months with me by invitation, a real bother, as was also the daughter of good Deacon Jones, who lived in our neighborhood a year and then went to his wild lands in Fulton County. Mrs. Jones asked me to keep her daughter and attend to her lessons, and accept her services as nurse for Charley and general assistant about the house in return. She stayed not quite a year, and home seemed better after she left. Rosetta Townsend spent much of her time with me; a lovely girl, and we all became warmly attached to her. A sadness rests on her memory. Her life was a short one—she was loving and amiable.

In the summer of 1826 we became members of the Shoal Creek Church in Bond County and Charles and John were baptized there, but as the church was sixteen miles from us we did not go to it only on communion seasons. It was the custom at that time to have the preparatory lecture on the Friday previous to the communion, and continue the services through Saturday, and as the log church was not convenient for a large gathering tents were put up, and such accommodations as are provided at Methodist camp meetings. Our other church priviliges were to go occasionally to the Methodist, Cumberland Presbyterian, or "Hard-shell" Baptist, none of which edified or spiritualized much. Our attempt to get up a Sunday school by inviting the children of the settlement to our house on Sunday was in some respects encouraging, though there were some drawbacks and discouragements attending it. One girl, whose father and mother could read, had instructed their promising daughter in all that they knew. She came a few Sundays, and because I would not give her lessons in grammar concluded that she could read as well as

I could, and so absented herself from the school. Sometimes I was sadly in doubt as to how to manage with the fathers and mothers of the children, who had never "seed" a Sunday-school, and came, bringing their babies, to sit as spectators while we gave instruction, but did not get ready to go away when the school was dismissed, and not until they had tasted the worth of Yankee cooking.

You may feel that I have attached undue notice to the meals given and the calls on our hospitality, but could you know the labor of bringing from raw materials anything at all presentable for family use, you would understand why the impression was so lasting. Besides the burden of cooking, there were many others. Every Monday morning, instead of pumping out a boiler of soft water, the kettle had to be suspended over the fire by means of pot-hooks fastened to a trammel that was suspended from a bar in the chimney. The getting the kettle hung was too severe for a woman's muscle, and a man had to be called into the performance. Then a small kettle containing ashes and water must also be put on the fire; when the small kettle boiled and the water became lye, it was taken off and settled as you would a pot of coffee; not with egg, but with cold water. When the large kettle of water boiled, the water from the small kettle must be dipped into it and stirred until flakes like snowflakes came up, and then, as Mother Seward—

who instructed me in the process—would say, "the water was broke." The scum was then taken off from the top and the water dipped into tubs to cool, a thick sediment would fall to the bottom of the tubs, leaving the water clean and pure, ready for use. As several kettles full had to pass through this process, it would occupy the first half of washing day, thereby bringing everything wrong. When the clothes were washed I, contrary to all rule among my neighbors, hung them on a line instead of the fence, but as clothes-pins were not known there, had to wait until I could find Loomis in the right mood to whittle some out, which, after about three months, he accomplished. The first time they were used I was attracted to the window to see what was the source of such jollification as was being shown by two of our backwoods neighbors. They were looking at the clothes yard, and calling to the third, who was on his way to join them, "See here, ain't that jest the last Yankee fixin'? jest see them ar little boys ridin' on a rope."

We had no market and must live as did our neighbors on corn bread and "flitch." "Flitch" was the fat portion of the hog, which would be laid on the floor in one corner of their smoke-house, and salt sprinkled over it; it was a filthy process, and when cooked (fried) was a disgusting food; so in order to have more comfortable fare ourselves, and to have something in readiness for the visitors that so unceremoniously came upon us, I had recourse to all the poor wits I possessed. We usually had a quarter of beef — nothing less — brought at a time; sometimes a whole animal. Your father knew nothing about cutting and dividing meat, so by the help of directions laid down in a cookery book and a little saw I attempted this art. When I could not manage among the big bones I would enlist your Uncle Robert, and we performed wonderfully. A part would be salted down to be used for corn beef when the fresh had been eaten; the pieces for roast and steak set apart; the fat about the kidneys carefully picked out and put to dry for suet, and the remainder of the fat melted, strained, and put away for candles; a part made into "collared" or "pressed beef;" the round made into "hunter's beef," and the shins hung up in a cool place for soup; so in attending to the different ways of disposing of these things I had plenty to do, to say nothing of the care required in warm weather to keep the flies from leaving a deposit whereby animal life was engendered.

But the most tedious thing was candle-making. Each desk in the office must be supplied with two candles, and with what was necessary for other parts of the house not less than three dozen would suffice for a week. Unfortunately for my own comfort I had experimented and made improvements in dipped candles until I had succeeded in getting them of such brilliancy that no others were to be used in the office. I used to dip sixteen dozen in the fall and twenty dozen in the spring. For the spring candles I boiled the tallow in alum water to harden it for summer use. Were I to attempt to tell you the process, or the labor bestowed on these "nocturnal luminaries," you would not comprehend it, and as the day is past for making them, being a part of housekeeping, it will not be worth while to expatiate further on their merits. But oh! I can fancy my poor, tired shoulder and strained arm are now in sympathy with the toil of tallow. Not like practicing two hours on the piano, which when you are tired you can stop, but from three to four mortal hours the right arm must be in constant movement. If a rest is given to the arm the candles become too hard and break, and the tallow in the pot gets too cool, so dip, dip, dip, six candles at a time; each time the candles grow heavier and heavier, and the shoulder more rebellious. Besides the dipped candles I had moulds in which I could mould two dozen at once, and all the accumula-ations from the beef that we weekly cooked was turned into moulded candles, which your father said looked well, but did not give as clear a light as his office candles. I sometimes bought a cake of deer's tallow; it was harder than beef, but not as white; the natives used to put beeswax in their tallow. I tried it, but found they emitted an unpleasant smoke.

Do not think that in all the four and a half years we sojourned at the farm, with all the disagreeable and laborious duties that devolved upon me, there were no bright spots — no silver linings to the lonely clouds. My two boys were real gems, relieving me of many lonely hours. We, too, had the acquaintance of the best people all over the state, and received visits from the most prominent men in the West.

In 1835 we were in Philadelphia, where Governor Coles had established himself after his marriage. He called with his wife to invite us to a party at his house. We there met the *élite* of the city, besides some distinguished strangers, and the Governor, when I alluded to our log cabin acquaintance, took occasion to inform the group that was near us that I had no claim to such a life; that I lived in a nicely painted house with a picket fence around it, and entertained more company than any other lady in the state. The old Governor was a little soft-soapy, and besides did not see our house until after it had received a covering of clapboards and a coat of white paint. I had many trials of patience within those old log walls and also many, very many things to alleviate the trials of backwoods life. Your father was in good business and had the means of doing many things for others less favored than himself. He had not only the means but the will to be generous, and he was certainly a most *cheerful giver*. It is one of the greatest comforts to me in looking back on the past that we were placed in a condition to extend favors to others, and if the means have been restricted, the will to do so is as strong as when the privilege was ours. I sometimes feel that if I had done more my restrictions would be less, but I hope never to live unmindful of the blessings that surrounded me in early life, and now that I am old and gray-headed I am not forsaken.

In the spring of 1827 we started from our western home to visit our kinsfolks, — a great event and a great undertaking. I had no nurse. Charley was three-and-a-half, and John a year-and-a-half old. Rosetta Townsend went with us and took care of Charles. He slept with her and she washed aud dressed him; but poor Johnnie! either the change of water or something else had given him a most inveterate summer sickness. It commenced at St. Louis and continued all the way. We were about four weeks in making the journey from St. Louis to Providence, an improvement in speed upon the seven-and-a-half weeks given to our first journey. I had had a winter of toil and moving with other labors attendant upon preparing for such a journey. My strength was so completely exhausted that but for the all-absorbing desire to go back to the home of my childhood I think my courage would have failed. Johnnie was a patient little sufferer all the way. But few were the nights of quiet rest for either of us.

We stopped a day or two at Louisville and Cincinnati, and at Pittsburgh took a stage for Erie, which was then a sorry little village. We waited three or four days for the lake to recover its smoothness after a long storm. The waves were rearing mountain high when we arrived there, and no boats ventured out for several days. We went to Buffalo, and started for Niagara the next morning. We were all day jolting over a wretched road in a carriage, a great part of the way through swampy ground with a corduroy bridging. The jolting was so severe on Johnnie that I carried him in my arms most of the way, and we did not reach Niagara until after dark, too late to see the Falls. As we were to leave the next day in time to reach and meet the canal boat, our only chance for seeing the Falls was to go out before breakfast; accordingly, as soon as the day dawned we were up, and leaving the children in bed, went out and feasted our eyes on the wonders of nature, returning to the hotel in time for breakfast and to hurry ourselves off for another corduroy siege.

At ——— we took the canal boat to ———, and then went by stage to Albany, where we stopped several days. Your father had business, and we found ourselves looking so decidedly shabby that we thought it the part of decency, at least, to make ourselves a little more presentable before reaching New York, where we expected to meet acquaintances. So

A Woman's Story

I had made a new, blue ladies' cloth traveling dress, a skirt and jacket, much as they are now worn, minus overskirt, a black figured silk dress, a leghorn bonnet, and some things for the children. Your father appeared in a new suit and much to our amusement the clerk, who had seen him go out and in for several days without making any particular demonstration, met him at the door as he came in the first time in his new suit, and with his most obsequious bow showed him to the best parlor, thinking he had a new guest. We went to New York and stayed with Rosetta's grandfather, Mr. Downing. It was easier for me, as I could leave the children with Rosetta and go out occasionally. I felt quite at home, and had an opportunity to get some rest. From New York we went to Providence and spent a few days, and then your Aunt Maria, taking little Maria, went with us to Kingston, where we all spent the rest of the summer.

Index

Index

ADAMS, John Quincy, appointments, 90-91.
Adamson, Miss —, married, 88.
Ague. See Fever and Ague.
Albany (N. Y.), visited, 153.
Allen, George C., pioneer, 7, 10.
Allen, Rowland P., pioneer, 7, 10.
Allen, Seth, at Providence, 34.
Alton, college at, 4; residents, 9.
American Fur Company, Illinois traders, xiii.
Amherst (Mass.), publication at, XX, 3.
Anti-slavery issue, in Illinois, 8, 9, 10, 137.   See also
   slavery.
Atlas, in Pike County, 7, 9.
Attleboro (Mass.), emigrant from, 95.
BALTIMORE, seaport, 11.
Baptists, in Illinois, 14, 78, 111-113, 146.
Barrens (Ky.), emigrants from, 25.
Barter, in early Illinois, 124, 130.
Bateman and Selby. *Historical Encyclopedia of Illi-
   nois*, xviii.
Bedford (Mass.), carriage factory at, 31.
Beef, bought by the quarter, 149.
Belleville, resident, 138.
Berry, Elijah C., auditor, 142.
Berry, William, state printer, 8.
Bird, —, brickmaker, 116, 118.
Birge, —, Greenville postmaster, 16, 72, 85.
Black, James, pioneer, 7, 73-74, 85, 95, 115, 117, 121;
   at Vandalia, 142.
Blackwell, Robert, pioneer, 7; sketch, 8-9.
Blunehard, Elisha, pioneer, 7.
Blanchard, Samuel, pioneer, 7.
Blanchard, Seth, pioneer, 7.

157

Index

Blanchard family, at Greenville, 16, 71-72, 85, 142.
Blane, William Newnham. *Excursion through the United States and Canada*, 34.
Bond County, settled, xiii, 13; divided, 15; county seat, 71; meeting in, 117, 120; church in, 146.
Bonhomme (Mo.), residents, 10.
Boston, port of departure, 11; interest in Illinois, 15-16; shopping in, 38; emigrants from, 41, 134.
Boston Medical College, professor, 5.
Boston *Recorder*, editor, 42.
Bowling Green (Ky.), law office at, 12.
Braley, Andrew, married, 11.
Braley, Eliza, mother, 128.
Breath, Edward, missionary, 142.
Breath, James, sketch, 10.
Breath family, pioneers, 7, 88, 142.
Brick-making, in Illinois, 115-116, 126-128.
Bridgewater (Mass.), Academy, students, 5.
Briggs, Mrs. —, grandmother of Mrs. Tillson, 31.
Briggs, Charles, Harvard graduate, 16.
Bright, Mrs. —, at St. Louis, 99-100.
Brown, William H., pioneer, 7, 117, 120; wife, 75, 86 117, 120; sketch, 8.
Buffalo (N. Y.), visited, 153.
Buzan, Billy, rents farm, 72; mentioned, 123.
Buzan, Jesse, pioneer, xvii, 27, 74, 81-84, 95, 98, 122, 144.
Buzan, Mrs. Jesse, visitor, 122-123.
Caleb, slave, 129, 134-136; desires manumission, 136-138; sketch, 138-141.
Cairo (Ill.), at mouth of Ohio, 46.
Calhoun, early name for Springfield, 90.
Calhoun County, settled, xii, 19.
California, gold rush, 9.
Candle-making, 97, 100, 149-150.
Canton, settler, 12.
Carlyle, visited, 70-71.
Carver, Jonathan, land grant, 21.
Carver (Mass.), emigrant from, 17, 73.
Caucus, in New York, 35.

Index

Chelsea (Mass.), residents, 5.
Chicago, portage at, xiii; early settlers, 8, 10, 75, 95.
Chicago Historical Society, xx.
Chicago Theological Seminary, building, 21.
Chillicothe (Ohio), route via, 33, 39; hotel at, 37.
Cincinnati, residents, 31, 36, 90; route via, 32-33; visited, 41, 43-44, 153.
Clarksville (Mo.), river town, 21.
Clay, Henry, relatives, 108.
Clemens, Mr. —, at St. Louis, 92.
Clermont County (Ohio), crossed, 33.
Clinton County, settled, xiii; seat, 70.
Coffey, —, Hillsboro pioneer, 15.
Coles, Edward, pioneer, 7; liberates slaves, 136; gubernatorial campaign, 137; in Philadelphia, 151; sketch, 9.
Collins, Almira, married, 94.
Collins, Augustus, pioneer, 7, 29-30, 53; sketch, 7.
Collins family, remove West, 29-30; visited, 142.
Collinsville, settled, 7-8, 30; visited, 142.
Columbus (Ohio), route via, 33.
Connecticut, emigrants from, 7, 29, 90, 93; travel through, 34.
Conover, —, in Illinois legislature, 77.
Cook, Daniel P., pioneer editor, 8.
Cook County, named, 8.
Cotton, raised in Illinois, 106-107.
Court week, in Illinois, 111-112.
Cox, Thomas, pioneer, 90.
Cumberland (Md.), route via, 33, 36.
Cumberland Presbyterians, in Illinois, 78, 146.
Cushman, Joshua, of Maine, 39.
Cushman, Joshua Jr., in Ohio, 31, 36, 39-41.
Cushman, Mrs. Jotham, accompanies Mrs. Tillson, 31, 33, 36, 42; incident concerning, 37-38; arrives at her son's, 40-41; sketch, 39.
DANFORTH, Joseph, in Louisville, 45.
Danforth, Joseph Jr., 45.
Danforth, Julia, 45.
Des Plaines River, trade route, xiii.

Index

Furniture, for log cabin, 98-100.
Fur trade, in Illinois, xiii.
GALENA, residents, xix, 7, 8, 10, 16.
Gallatin County, salines in, xii.
Germans, in Pennsylvania, 35-36; in Illinois, 110.
Giddings, Mrs. Almira, pioneer, 29-30.
Giddings, Frederic, born, 30; at Quincy, 94.
Gillett, Mrs. Dr., of Jacksonville, 29.
Grant, Mrs. Ulysses S., married, 45.
Greene County, settled, xii.
Greenville, early settlers, 7, 16, 71-72, 75, 85; post
   office at, 16; brick making, 116; physician, 132;
   visited, 142.
HALIFAX (Mass.), emigrants from, xvii, xix, 4, 11, 31,
   39, 124.
Hablet, Moses, pioneer, 11-12, 15, 28.
Hamilton, William S., pioneer, 7; sketch, 9.
Hamilton. See Hillsboro.
Hanna, Brice, pioneer, xvii, 69, 89; visited, 51, 55,
   57-68.
Hanson (Mass.), 39.
Hardy, —, Presbyterian minister, 56.
Hartford (Conn.), resident, 93.
Harvard College, graduate, 16.
Hatch, —, Springfield pioneer, 91.
Havana, settled, 22.
Henry (Ill.), early settler, 10.
Hillsboro, settlers, xvii, 10, 12, 17; natives, xviii-xix;
   county seat, 15, 125; Tillsons move to, 125-128.
Hillsboro Academy, founder, xvii.
Hilton, —, Shawneetown landlord, 50.
Hinckley, Mrs. Julia Townsend, 9-10; as a child, 128,
   133.
Hind's Prairie, in Illinois, 65.
Holmes, Ellen, married, 101.
Home manufactures, 24-26. See also Candle making.
Hopkins, Major —, hotel keeper, 88, 143.
Hopkins, Polly, at Edwardsville, 88.
Horn, —, farm hand, 114.
Hough, Emerson, *The Passing of the Frontier*, xvi.

Index

Index

Index

Index

Index

Index

Kay J. Carr teaches American history at Southern Illinois University at Carbondale. She received her B.A. degree in history from Knox College and her M.A. and Ph.D. degrees in history from the University of Chicago. Previous publications include: *The Illinois and Michigan Canal Heritage Corridor: A Guide to Its History and Sources* (edited, with Michael P. Conzen); and "Community Dynamics and Educational Decisions: Establishing Public Schools in Belleville and Galesburg," which received the Harry E. Pratt Memorial Award as the best article in Illinois history in 1991. Her scholarly interests include the history and geography of Illinois and the Midwest.

Shawnee Classics

A Series of Classic Regional Reprints for the Midwest

"Black Jack"
John A. Logan and Southern Illinois
    in the Civil War Era
James Pickett Jones

A Woman's Story of Pioneer Illinois
Christiana Holmes Tillson
Edited by Milo Milton Quaife